The Briefcase and The Baby

Angela Holford has worked as a nanny for ten years since qualifying as an NNEB Nursery Nurse at Eastbourne College in 1981; she also holds the PreSchool Playgroup Association Certificate and studied psychology at evening classes for three years. She has been a supervisor of a playgroup, worked in summer playschemes and once set up a nanny friendship group, 'Nannies Anonymous'. She has looked after all combinations and ages of children, living both in and out, has worked in the town and country and abroad on family holidays, and has had both good and bad experiences in her jobs.

Amanda Cuthbert is a writer and producer of television programmes for children; she is a working mother with two sons – a four-year-old and a nine-year-old (who gave up onion bhajias for Lent when he was six). She employed her first nanny four weeks after the first was born and has employed nannies, both good and bad, qualified and unqualified, live-in and live-out, throughout their childhood, during which time she has worked both in an office and from home, and travelled abroad.

Angela worked for Amanda for two years before they started work on *The Briefcase and the Baby*, and they maintained this working relationship whilst they wrote it, juggling jobs, children and computers.

The Briefcase and The Baby

A Nanny and Mother's Handbook

AMANDA CUTHBERT
and
ANGELA HOLFORD
with illustrations by Ros Asquith

Mandarin

A Mandarin Paperback
THE BRIEFCASE AND THE BABY

First published in Great Britain 1992
by Mandarin Paperbacks
Michelin House, 81 Fulham Road, London sw3 6rb

Mandarin is an imprint of the Octopus Publishing Group,
a division of Reed International Books Limited

Copyright © 1992 by Amanda Cuthbert and Angela Holford
Illustrations copyright © 1992 by Ros Asquith

A CIP catalogue record for this title
is available from the British Library
isbn 0 7493 0967 9

Printed and bound in Great Britain
by Cox & Wyman Ltd, Reading, Berks

To Joel and Luke,
without whom this would not have been written.

Contents

Acknowledgements

We would like to thank the following people for their part in *The Briefcase and the Baby*:

Chad and Steve for coping in our absence and giving us time, space and cups of tea when we flagged; Brian Haynes for acting as midwife; Shan Morley Jones, Jane Carr, Sheila, George and Michael Holford, and Margaret Horne for their continuous support and encouragement; Sandra Holland, Liz Hawken, and Dee Stovold for acting as nannies when time got short; Kath Bird for her help and for unravelling the mysteries of the computer; Aslan, for walking all over it.

And all those friends, both nannies and employers, who gave us their time and filled in our questionnaires, particularly Nina Acton and Bridgette James.

Introduction

- She was good for the first two months but now her standards have dropped.
- I've told her I don't like them having sweets but I find sweet papers in the car.
- She never washes the grill pan.

- I was told at the interview I would be doing occasional babysitting and now it is four nights a week.
- I never know whether I'm expected to eat with them or not.
- I always have to ask for my wages.

The Briefcase and the Baby is a handbook for nannies and those who employ them; in it we have tackled all the issues of importance to both sides, from how to handle an interview to who should look after the plumber. We have tried to help you to deal with those little things that, if left unattended to, add up to major sources of conflict in the nanny/employer situation.

In *The Briefcase and the Baby*, for the first time, both nanny and mother have a voice in the same book, giving each a unique insight into how the other thinks and feels.

This is a book for nannies, those of you who are training to be nannies and those of you who, qualified or unqualified, are already in jobs. It is for anyone who is employed by a family to look after their children who feels in need of guidance or reassurance, and it is to help you make nannying work for you, your employer and the children you care for.

This book is for the many harassed, guilt-ridden mothers who employ nannies, whether for the first time or not, whose experiences have been baffling, frustrating and disheartening. It is intended to help you handle your nannies and understand them better and so treat them in a way which will make for easier relationships all round.

Through writing this book at the same time as having an employer/employee relationship, we have had to tackle painful and funny subjects in a totally honest way, which has meant examining our motives (both good and bad) and confronting issues which we had previously avoided. We have spent many hours talking about the joys and problems of working as/ employing a nanny; the results of those conversations are in this book.

Nannying is unique in the employment field: when your workplace is also your home and when your employee lives as part of the family the physical balance of power is totally in the employer's favour (the nanny is on her own in the employer's home, often relying on her entirely for food and shelter as well as for wages and terms and conditions; she can therefore be reluctant to create problems which might affect these). But the emotional balance of power is totally in the nanny's favour (the nanny looks after the most important part of her employer's life — her child — and the employer will not want to upset her in case she takes it out on her child or leaves, thus causing the child upset and herself more guilt).

The Briefcase and the Baby addresses this unique situation and aims to:

- Encourage communication, awareness and give-and-take between mother and nanny, helping you to establish a good relationship from the beginning, built on respect and understanding of the constraints, pressures and problems of both sides.
- Help you to be assertive when confronting difficult issues that need resolving, and still keep the relationship friendly.

- Help you to be one step ahead and to recognise and deal with possible problems early on.
- Encourage you to approach employing/working as a nanny in a professional manner and to treat the situation like a conventional job within the limits of the domestic environment.
- Give support to nannies and mothers — particularly those dealing with the situation for the first time.

Throughout this book:

 = The nanny's voice   = The working mother's voice

- We have assumed that nannies are 'live-in' for the purpose of the book, but most of the advice also applies to 'live-out' nannies.
- Cross-references to other relevant subjects are listed at the end of each section under 'See Also'.
- Addresses: where the organisations have their headquarters in London, we have listed the London address, which can be contacted for details of any local offices.
- To the best of our knowledge all information is correct at the time of going to press.

Accidents

Minor accidents are inevitable with children and as a nanny you are in a particularly vulnerable position, since you probably look after the children for more hours per week than anyone else. As the children are not yours, the responsibility before the accident and the guilt after it are greater than if the children were your own.

If you are consistently meticulous with safety precautions in every area of your work, you will reduce the possibility of accidents and not feel quite so bad when they happen.

In the first few days in your job find out:

- The addresses and telephone numbers of employers' workplaces, grandparents, a local close friend of the family, the family doctor, the local police station and the children's schools.
- Where the first aid and first aid book is kept in the house.
- The route to the doctor's surgery and the hospital.

If the child in your care has a minor accident, you will have to decide on the treatment needed. In most cases you will be able to deal with the problem yourself.

When an accident happens which you do not feel able to cope with properly, get help as fast as you can and get the child to a doctor or hospital. Stay with the child. If necessary and possible, arrange care for the other children in your charge. It is important to tell whoever is treating the child that you are the nanny.

Whether the accident is minor or major it is important that you inform the parents exactly what happened and what you have done about it. This may not be easy. *You* know how and why the accident happened, but somehow putting it into words makes it sound worse than it was. If you tell the truth, and all is well, the parents will be grateful that you were capable and coped. Your attitude to the accident will affect your employers' attitude to you.

If the accident is a serious one your guilt may be so great that you will want to leave the job; if your employers want you to stay, consider it. Staying in the job will help the child and the family recover, and you will have the opportunity to make amends and alleviate your guilt.

There is a temptation to feel that 'accidents happen, but not when I'm in charge'; if there is an accident involving your children when in your nanny's care you may feel shocked, angry with your nanny, and possibly yourself for not having been there when it happened. It will help if you ask yourself:

- Is anyone hurt? How badly?
- Is it your nanny's fault?
- Could it have been avoided with better care, planning, and professionalism? Or is it a genuine accident?
- Is your nanny unconcerned?
- Is this one of many accidents?
- Do you now distrust your nanny with your children/ house/car?

If the answer to all these questions is 'no' then the accident is probably best forgiven and forgotten and appropriate action taken to prevent any future recurrence.

If the accident seriously affects your children you will probably find it hard to trust the nanny with them in the future, unless it was clearly not her fault. Consider her record with you to date and think of her feelings as well as your own. She may lose confidence and want to leave.

If the accident is due to your nanny's carelessness and is one of several recent unfortunate events you may need to look at how well your nanny is coping in general; if she is becoming slapdash, has she come to the end of her real interest in the job? If so, you would do well to discuss it with her. Whilst it is a rare nanny who will actually tell you that she wants to move on, it is obviously better to face the possibility sooner rather than later from both points of view.

> *Maria's three-year-old son swallowed half a bottle of his nanny's pills which she had left within his reach. Maria rushed him to hospital and, after a frightening two days, she took him home again to be greeted by a guilt-stricken and intensely apologetic nanny. Maria asked the nanny to leave. Looking back Maria realised that her nanny's mind had not been on the job for a few weeks — she had burned a hole in the ironing and let the bath overflow twice in the same week. The nanny had put Maria in an impossible situation and whilst she did not want to sack her, her trust in her was gone and she could not let her stay.*

You may want to consider taking out an insurance policy to cover all eventualities.

See also: Cars, Insurance, Safety

Althea, *Be Careful* (Dinosaur).
Children teach their teddies to avoid accidents.
ROSPA endorsed.

The British Red Cross, *Practical First Aid* (Dorling Kindersley).

The Royal Society for the Prevention of Accidents,
Cannon House, The Priory,
Queensway, Birmingham B46 BS1
Tel: 021 200 2461
Advice, leaflets, books and videos.

Activities

There are many different forms of activity — this section covers those which can be done at home.

Encouraging children to do many varied activities shows a good attitude to your job. Your employers will be pleased as it shows them that their children are being stimulated and are learning while in your care; also, it makes the time go more quickly for you.

Before starting an activity make sure it is suitable for the age and ability of the child. Check that you have the right equipment and materials and the time and space to do the activity. Afterwards involve the children in clearing up and displaying the results. If you plan to do something that is new, costly, or in any way dangerous, ask your employer first.

There are endless sources of ideas from the many books and television programmes that exist, to more unusual sources like garden and leisure centres (where you can find project ideas, craft kits, weather charts, activity sheets, etc.). There is a vast range of activities that you can do at home with your charges, including ball games, cooking, craft work, cutting and sticking, dressing up, gardening, junk modelling, music, movement and drama, painting, puppet shows, treasure hunts, scrap books, sewing, and play with water, sand, dough, and gravel or rice trays.

Quick Tip: Keep a record of any activities which you know are successful so that you can call upon them as and when needed.

Some working mothers feel that they are missing out on the chance to do creative things with their children. You may well be too tired/busy at the weekends when the children are around to spend much creative time with them, or you may infinitely prefer the challenge of the work place to the challenge of a small child's imagination — which may make you feel guilty! One of the big advantages of employing a good nanny is that she is good at creative play and has the time to indulge in it to the full.

A common complaint is that your child seems to spend more time at coffee mornings or in front of the television set than doing something creative with the nanny. You will naturally want your children to be stimulated, educated and entertained and may hope that your nanny will spend a large part of the day doing just this. She won't! If she is to be content working for you she needs a social life and time for the washing, ironing and cooking as well. Balance is the key: television, coffee mornings and shopping are fine and offer learning situations in their own way if balanced with creative activities and a loving attitude.

Be realistic in your expectations, make clear what you would like, and be appreciative of your nanny's efforts.

See also: Group activities, outings

Dorothy Einon, *Creative Play* (Penguin).
For adults. Explains play, gives ideas.

Melanie Rice, *Play Together Learn Together* (Kingfisher).
Lots of make and do ideas.

McPhee Gribble *The Puffin Do It Yourself Book* (Puffin).
Imaginative ideas for make and do.

There are many books published by Usborne covering a wide range of activities.

Adoption

If your children are adopted, your nanny should be told at the interview stage, along with any other information that you feel will be useful to her — their history, perhaps, and how much they know and understand about their adoption.

If you decide to add to your existing family by adopting a child you will need to discuss it fully with your nanny; do not assume that she will want to take on another child. This may be the moment to review her terms and conditions, or possibly to find a new nanny.

In either case you will need to co-ordinate your approach to answering the children's questions and dealing with any problems.

If you have a job with adopted children it may help you to understand their feelings and explain things to them if you have found out as much information as possible; if you can, talk to nannies who have worked in similar situations, people who are adopted, and parents who have adopted and brought up children.

If, once you are working for a family, they decide to adopt a child, you will need to prepare the existing children for the new arrival and to work closely with the parents. You will need to agree on how you will handle the new situation, for example helping the existing children accept their new sibling and dealing with any rivalry or behavioural problems between the natural and the adopted children.

See also: Questions

Susan Lapsley, *I Am Adopted* (Bodley Head).
For children of five years plus; help with facts/concepts.

Explaining Adoption (B.A.A.F.).
Explaining to children why they are adopted.

Family Talk (B.A.A.F.).
Pack of information, with worksheets for children whose families are adopting or fostering. Addresses and books and games to play.

British Agencies for Adoption and Fostering
11 Southwark Street,
London SE1 1RQ
Tel: 071 407 8800.
A source of information and advice. Useful addresses, agencies.

Advances

There is no future in responding to advances from any member of the family you are working for. Due to the nature of a nannying job, working and living closely with other adults in a home environment, you have to be able to recognise and rebuff advances and not do or say anything that could be interpreted as an advance.

If you think that someone is making advances to you and this is worrying you, before you act ask yourself:

- Are you leading them on?
- Is it a one-off?
- Is he/she just being friendly?
- Are you over-reacting?
- Is he/she leaving soon?

If the answer to all of these is 'no' you will have to do something about the situation. Initially the easiest way of dealing with it is to treat it as a joke, but make it clear that you are not interested.

If this does not work then you will have to ask him/her to stop directly. You could tell another member of the family who may be able to help you; however, be prepared for them not to believe or support you — it may be too difficult for them to do so.

You may end up in the situation of being asked to leave, or find that if you stay it is difficult to carry on working in that job. You may decide it is best to give another reason for leaving and arrange to do so.

If you got the job through an agency, tell them what happened to protect the next nanny.

Emma worked for a family where the mother was a nurse working nights. Without warning one night she woke to find the father getting into bed with her. She only managed to stop him by threatening to call the police. He then stood and watched her as she packed and left the house within an hour.

This is another of those situations which is exacerbated by the fact that the nanny is at work in her home; office intrigues and sexual exploits take place away from home and can therefore be handled discreetly if this is necessary. Office workers also have some sort of protection in law for sexual harassment, and like as not colleagues around to witness it and help. If a member of the family makes advances to the nanny she has no support, her job is threatened and she cannot escape from her pursuer in the evenings.

It is very easy for male members of the family to take advantage of having an extra female in the house without even realising it, and to behave in a way which they would not dream of doing at the office; it is important for them to be aware that their actions are open to being misinterpreted as advances. They must respect the nanny's privacy.

There is obviously a world of difference between friendliness and overt sexual innuendo and every situation is different; however, if your husband makes serious advances to your nanny you can choose to get rid of him or her, for the sake of the children, the nanny and yourself.

There are several stories of nannies quietly worshipping the ground their male employer walks on; at best your husband will be flattered, his ego stroked and no harm done. If however, your nanny makes advances to your husband show her the door. Do not give her a reference and report her to the agency if you got her through one.

> *Laura had only been in her new job a few weeks when she became very concerned over Richard, the father's behaviour. After her evenings out she would return to her room to find a pair of his boxer shorts on her bed. She decided to ignore this, not to react, but to return them unseen to the laundry basket. It was on one such occasion that the mother caught her in the act and asked her what she was doing. Laura was terrified but managed to reply, 'Nothing — just putting some of the baby's clothes out for washing.' 'That's OK then,' said the mother, 'only I thought for a moment that the dog had been bringing you Richard's clothes like she did with our old nanny.'*

See also: Fathers

 Rape Crisis Centre,
PO Box 69,
London WC1
Tel: 071 837 1600 (24-hour)
    071 278 3956 (Office)
Offers support and advice for victims of rape or sexual abuse.

Syd Hoare, *Teach Yourself Self-Defence* (Hodder and Stoughton).
Simple techniques with illustrations.

Advertisements

 When you are struggling to squeeze your advertisement into twenty words and spending hours trying to make you and yours sound intriguing and fun:

Do:
- Include your basic requirements, worded as briefly as possible, e.g. type of nanny, number, age and sex of children, hours, nursery/household duties, driver, smoking or non-smoking, experienced or not, trained or not, anything specific.
- Say what you have to offer to attract the prospective nanny, e.g. accommodation (self-contained, bathroom, television, etc.), time off, use of car, foreign holidays, swimming pool, luxury jet!
- Put your telephone number rather than your address or a box number if you want a quick response and a choice; most nannies prefer to telephone.
- Be specific about the times to ring if you do not want your current nanny to answer the calls for you.
- State what area you live in; this is important to a nanny who cannot tell from your telephone number alone.

Don't:
- Include salary; you may wish to negotiate this depending on the age, qualifications and experience of the interviewee.
- Put the names of your children in the advert.
- Gush! Your adorable children can be bloody with others and what you consider to be a cosy home may be claustrophobic to someone else.

You can give the feel of you and your family in the advertisement through careful choice of words; for example, asking for a cheerful and reliable nanny is more friendly than asking for an efficient and sensible one, and writing 'Help, we are desperate! gives a disorganised, emotional tone compared to 'urgently required'.

You may well be in a panic when you place your advertisement — nannies often give notice suddenly. It is worth paying for two consecutive weeks since if you do not and the first week fails to produce a nanny, you will be losing time. The following are possible places to advertise:

The Lady. Eight days' lead time, or fifteen days if you miss the deadline. Not so useful for those in a hurry, but the bible for anyone looking for a job as a nanny, qualified or unqualified.

Nursery World. One week's lead time. A magazine for nursery nurses — good for finding more mature, qualified and experienced nannies.

Local paper. Usually a short lead time and good for finding a local nanny or a mum whose children are grown and who wants to work.

Local shop. If you place a card in the windows, be wary about how much information you put on it — don't give the local burglar your address and telephone number!

Be wary of the nanny network as a way of replacing an old nanny — it has been known for a nanny to take a job to get her friend out of a fix and then hand in her notice six weeks later.

If you want a college leaver, write to a local college and advertise in April/May for the nanny to join in June. Some newly qualified nannies will take a holiday and look for a job afterwards, so July and August are also good times. Few nannies change jobs at Christmas time, which can make it a bad time to advertise.

Once you have placed the advertisement, keep a list of essential questions by the phone so that you can instantly weed out the nannies who do not have the basic qualities you are looking for. This helps you avoid long fruitless telephone conversations and reduces the number of embarrassing interviews later.

Keep a chart by the phone for the nannies' details with name, age, telephone number, qualifications, experience, age and sex of children she has cared for and miscellaneous sections; this can be invaluable after two hours on the phone when all the nannies have merged into one.

The first step in the chain of job-hunting. Adverts can tell you a lot about the job. The most obvious places to look for adverts which cover both the United Kingdom and abroad are *The Lady* or *Nursery World*. If you wish to work locally, the local papers, shops and clinics may be more useful.

Before contacting a prospective employer, decide what your basic requirements are and where you are prepared to be flexible. You will want to think about whether you are prepared to live in or out, the type of job you are qualified for and require, the areas you would consider working in and anything else that is important to you, such as the number of children, the hours and the duties. Once you have decided these you will be able to weed out the unsuitable jobs and avoid pointless telephone calls.

Having found some suitable adverts:

- Write down what you want to know — have pen and paper ready. Do not just ask about the perks, show interest in the children too.
- Ring at stated times.
- Have your first line ready, for example, 'Hello, I am ringing about your advert for a nanny in the *Daily News* on Friday.'
- Have your c.v. nearby; this will act as a reminder when you are asked a lot of questions.

Advertising Yourself. If you are having difficulty finding exactly what you want, you may consider advertising yourself. Choose a 'situations wanted' column in a local paper/magazine with a good number of readers. You will need to state your qualifications and/or experience, the type of work you want, whether it is live in or out, whether you are a non-smoker, driver, rider, swimmer, etc. Also state your age, references and a contact number.

Box Numbers. This means you can only contact or be contacted by letter. The advertiser has paid more for the privacy of using the paper's address. If you write for a job, be sure to enclose a full c.v. It is also a good idea to send a photograph of yourself, preferably with children.

 Quick Tip: If you do not like the tone of the advert the chances are you will not like the people who wrote it.

The Truth Is . . .

Attractive salary: *Pretty awful.*

Fashion model mother/TV personality father: *We love ourselves and our jobs.*

Help, help, help: *Playing for sympathy.*

Country loving: *We live miles from anywhere, with frequent power cuts and lots of mud.*

Sense of humour and energy essential: *Smile as you run.*

Must love babies: *Is that fried or grilled?*

Three gorgeous children: *Until they start to play mum off against nanny.*

Present nanny recommends: *The sooner you come the sooner she can go.*

David (9), Clare (5), Chloe (1), Dog (3): *Dog more trouble than children.*

Nanny, (min age 20): *19 years 11 months 362 days just won't do.*

Friendly informal household: *Chaos.*

Our present nanny has to leave (sigh): *Is that sadness or relief?*

Hi, I'm a lovable 8-month-old boy and I have a gorgeous sister age 5: *Pass the Rennies.*

Nanny/Mother's Help: *We would love a nanny, but can only afford a mother's help.*

Opportunity to decorate your own room: *The box room needs redecorating and we haven't got time.*

Flexible time off: *You fit around us, and we'll tell you when we can fit around you.*

Car at disposal of driver: *Please take to nearest tip.*

See Also: Agencies, Interviews

Nursery World,
Child Care Classified Department,
The SchoolHouse Workshop,
51 Calthorne Street,
London WC1X 0HH
Tel: 071 837 7224
Fax: 071 278 3896
Advertisements may be placed by post, telephone or fax and paid for by credit card.

The Lady,
The Classified Advertisement Dept,
39-40 Bedford Street,
London WC2E 9ER
Telephone instructions are not accepted.

Agencies

You may choose to use an agency — or several — to help you find a job/nanny; all agencies have to be registered by the Department of Employment and display their licence number and certificate at their premises. Agencies make their money through registration and placement fees charged to employers and these fees vary enormously from agency to agency, as does the quality of service offered. There are obviously advantages to joining an agency if you are prepared to fill in application forms and wait while they receive and process them.

Agencies can be found through *The Lady*, *Nursery World*, local and national newspapers and magazines, telephone books under 'Employment Agencies', college noticeboards and The Federation of Recruitment and Employment Services.

A *good* agency will offer guidelines on salaries and negotiate terms and conditions. It will check out both nannies and employers fully and help you avoid endless unsuitable interviews by careful matching of nanny and employer: it will sometimes also offer after-placement care and can be a good source of temporary nannies/jobs; it can also offer information and advice for a mother or nanny needing reassurance.

Not all agencies offer the same quality service. A common complaint from both employers and nannies is that agencies try to persuade them into unsuitable interviews; this is to be resisted at all costs since it is always a waste of time. Agencies are only going to make any money if they match a nanny with an employer, and the truth sometimes gets bent in the attempt.

 As a nanny, choosing a good agency can be difficult; here are eight questions worth considering:

1. What type of jobs do they have on their books at that moment? How many jobs are available? A wide variety and large number of jobs indicates a well-established agency.
2. Are they familiar with the area you want to work in? If not you may be offered interviews in inappropriate areas. This is particularly relevant if you are looking for a job in the country.
3. How do they vet their nannies? An agency which does not ask you to fill in a detailed application form and provide references is not worth considering. By law you are required to provide two references with up-to-date telephone numbers.

4. Do they interview you before sending you to a job interview? This is not always possible, but ideally they will.
5. Do they contact and negotiate with the employers for you or do they simply give you details and phone numbers? They should act on your behalf — that is the advantage of going to an agency.
6. Do they recommend contracts to both employer and nanny? Do they supply contracts?
7. Do they make sure your prospective employers are aware of the need to pay your national insurance and tax?
8. Do they offer after-placement care and advice, friendship circles and newsletters? It is a bonus if they do.

➡ Quick Tip: Have a passport-size photo ready — many agencies ask for this on the application form.

 Some employers prefer to use agencies to find their nannies in spite of the cost; with charges of anything up to 12 per cent of net annual salary and differing guarantee periods, your choice of agency will probably relate to your ability to pay and your state of desperation at the time. Some agencies also charge a nominal registration fee. Choosing an agency can be difficult — if possible, talk to other mothers for recommendations. If you have time, it is worth going to visit the agency. Otherwise, their attitude to you on the telephone will tell you a lot.

It is worthwhile finding out what the going rate is for nannies being offered similar terms and conditions to yours in your area, so that you can judge whether the salary the agency suggests is reasonable. The higher the salary, the larger the agency's fee.

It is also a good idea to ring several agencies for comparison of their services. You will want to ask them whether they interview the nanny in person, on the telephone, or merely read application forms; and also whether they follow up references. Agencies vary considerably in what they offer for their fee.

Have your job outline well defined when you telephone the

agency since they will be passing on your details to prospective nannies, and vague descriptions can be interpreted in a negative fashion.

Job Description	How the Agency Sees it
On Monday it's 8 am to 6 pm, on Tuesday 7.30 am to 9 pm, except once a month when it's 7.30 am to 10 pm; on Wednesday I work at home sometimes and then it's 9 am to 5 pm except when I'm called in, when it's 7.30 am to 6.30 pm. Thursdays is flexible, depending on my workload and Fridays it's 8 am to 6 pm, except when my husband is travelling, when I may need my nanny to stay the night.	This woman is all over the place; any nanny working here will be exploited, never know what she is doing from one day to the next. This will be a difficult job to sell to a nanny.

If the employer re-words her job description:

I need a nanny for a maximum of fifty hours per week, after which we pay overtime. I work the hours out with the nanny a week in advance, and these vary from week to week.	Not a conventional job but the employer is aware of the need for a set number of hours and the need to give the nanny notice of these in good time.

When you receive the agency's application form and terms and conditions it is advisable to examine the small print and establish exactly what you get for your money, for example, how long is the period during which they will replace a nanny if she proves unsuitable at no extra charge, and how many times will they do this? If there is a clause providing for this, remember that in practice they may not be able to replace a nanny with another one you like, in which case they may offer a partial refund.

You never know when you may need the services of an agency — it is a good idea to be one step ahead and have found one or two that you feel you can trust in case you do.

See Also: Advertisements, Interviews

A typical Job Application form looks like this:

ANGEE'S AGENCY WORKING FOR YOU!!   please affix a
                                                    recent photo of
                                                    yourself here.

PLEASE WRITE IN BLOCK CAPITALS

Name_____ Surname Mrs, Miss, Ms, Mr_____
Present Address_____
Home Address if different_____
Telephone No. Home_____ Work_____
Nationality_____ Religion_____
Marital Status_____
Date of birth_____ Age_____
Health, known allergies, disabilities_____

EDUCATION AND QUALIFICATIONS
Name of School_____
Qualifications_____
Further education_____
Qualifications_____

EMPLOYMENT DETAILS
Present: Name_____
Address_____
Brief description of job including children's ages_____
Previous: Name_____
Address_____
Brief description of job including children's ages_____

TYPE OF JOB YOU REQUIRE (please tick)
Nanny_____ Mother's Help_____ Maternity_____
Permanent_____ Temporary_____ Daily_____ Live in_____
Sole charge_____
Are you a_____ driver_____ smoker_____ swimmer_____ rider_____
Area required_____
Nursery duties only_____ Light housework_____ Housekeeper_____
Number of children preferred_____ Ages_____
SALARY REQUIRED_____
When are you free to start?_____

ADDITIONAL INFORMATION
Interests and Hobbies_____
Do you have any dependants?_____
Do you have a criminal record?_____
How did you hear of Angee's Agency?_____
Please give names and addresses of two references (not relatives)
Name_____ Name_____
Address_____ Address_____
I certify that this information is correct and true. I realise that any information given
to me about potential employers is highly confidential.
I will notify the agency if I obtain a job through the agency or by other means.
Signed_____ Date_____

FRES, The Federation of Recruitment and
Employment Services,
36-38 Mortimer Street,
London W1N 7RB
Tel: 071 323 4300
The trade association for private recruitment agencies,
including those who specialise in nannies and child
carers.

Department of Employment,
Agency Licensing Section,
2-16 Church Road,
Stanmore, Middlesex HA7 4AW
Tel: 081 954 7677
Contact this section of the department if you think an
agency has acted improperly.

Alcohol / Drugs

Being drunk while on duty is a sackable offence. Whilst
the occasional drink may not do any harm, too much
affects your ability to care for the children. If you are
offered a drink whilst on duty, just have one. You should never
drink and drive whilst in charge of your employers' car and
children.

You may well be offered a drink by your employers in the
evening when they come home; remember that you are still their
employee and whilst this is a good way to ease any tensions and
establish a friendly relationship, you may well regret offering to
clean the oven or telling them the intimate details of your Greek
holiday when you wake up the next day.

You have the right to choose whether or not you drink in your
free time, but will need to establish with your employers
whether or not you are allowed to do so in their house either on
your own or with friends.

Coming home drunk will not do you any favours with your

employers, especially if you do so regularly. If you have a hangover the next morning which causes you problems while you are working, your employer may well be annoyed and can even dismiss you, as your drinking affects your job.

> *One alcoholic employer had gone through several nannies who could not handle her drinking and behaviour when drunk. She took on an experienced nanny by chance who tackled the problem, which was affecting the child, by persuading her employer to seek treatment and helping her through it.*

Should your employer have a drink problem and it is affecting you and your job, you are in a very difficult situation. The children will probably feel insecure, confused and frightened if they see their parents under the influence of drink. You will need to reassure them and help them cope with it.

What you do about it will depend on the size of the problem and the type of job you are in. You could talk to the drinker's partner, offer support and help to the drinker and, at worst, leave.

If you, a friend or an employer need more help and advice you can contact a doctor or one of the organisations below.

> *One Wednesday I was changing the children's beds when there was a clunk and a bottle of whisky fell from between Joe's mattress and bed. A quarter was gone. When he came home, I asked him what he had been doing, where it had come from, and whether he had drunk any. He said he had tasted some but he had used the rest to make glue.*
>
> *I told him he must not take daddy's whisky or drink whisky and that whisky was very expensive and not for boys of seven.*
>
> *On the Friday he proudly told me at tea that he was being good. He was sorry he had taken the whisky. He had discovered that sherry made much better glue.*

You need to make your views on alcohol absolutely clear when your nanny starts working for you. Show her the door if she is drunk on duty; if she is not responsible with herself the chances are she is not responsible with your children.

If your nanny drinks so much in her leisure time that she is ill or unfit for work the next day you need to talk to her straight away. It can be overlooked if it only happens once but if it occurs frequently you are within your rights to ask her to leave.

Many employers reach for the bottle when they fall through the door in the evening and share a drink with their live-in nannies. Whilst it is good to relax informally with your nanny, beware of the fine line between friendly chat and over-confidentiality: whilst it may seem harmless to share family secrets when you are tired and tiddly it may not feel harmless living with the knowledge that your nanny knows something about you that you would rather she did not. At worst she may breach your confidentiality. It is unfair to burden your nanny with highly confidential information — the temptation to talk about things with other nannies over coffee is enormous.

If you yourself have a problem with alcohol you will affect both the children and the nanny; you are unlikely to find a nanny who can cope with your problem for very long, which will lead to a high turnover of nannies and unsettled children. Get help.

 Quick Tip: Remember to keep alcohol out of reach of the children at all times.

Claire Rayner, *The Don't Spoil Your Body Book* (Bodley Head).
Explains simply the effects of alcohol and other chemicals on the body and how to keep healthy.

Al-Anon & Alateen,
61, Great Dover Street,
London SE1 4YF
Tel: 071 403 0888
For those who are affected by other people's drinking.
Alateen is especially for younger people. Contact this
address to find out your local branch. Information,
books and leaflets supplied.

Alcoholics Anonymous,
PO Box 514,
11 Redcliffe Gardens,
London SW1 9BQ
Tel: 071 352 3001
0904 644026 (General Service Office)
Helpline from others who have had a drink problem
and want to help you give up alcohol.

Drugs

The above applies equally to the use of drugs; as with
alcohol, drugs and children do not mix.

Vanora Leigh, *Drugs: Why Say No?* (Penguin).
An informative guide.

SCODA Standing Conference on Drug Abuse,
1-4 Hatton Place,
London EC1N 8ND
Tel: 071 430 2341
Can put you in touch with your local organisations that
help users and their families.

Families Anonymous
310 Finchley Road,
London NW3
Tel: 071 731 8060
Can put you in touch with family help groups in your
area or help you set one up.

Babies

Finding and employing a nanny for your first baby can be nerve-racking; you have never done it before, you are unused to being a mother, you may not want to leave your child at all or you may not be able to afford the kind of nanny you would really like. It will help you if you are clear about the sort of qualities you require in a nanny to care for your baby.

Ideally she should have:

- experience of babies, particularly if she is to be in sole charge.
- a knowledge of what caring for babies involves and of the stages of development, e.g. weaning, sleeping, teething and so on.
- a genuine enjoyment of babies.

Whilst some mothers prefer to have the early weeks alone with their babies so that they get to know them and how to handle them without help, some employ their nanny before the birth to get her used to the family and help prepare for the arrival. If you are employing a nanny who has to give notice in another job, you will obviously need to agree and keep to a start date, regardless of whether or not your baby is born early or late.

Since the first weeks can be tearful, emotional and exhausting, having a nanny with you from the beginning can be very helpful — she can do everything except feed it, if you are breastfeeding, if you want her to. It also means that you can set up your routine as you want it with her. However, the period when you are both in the house together can be an awkward one; even if your relationship is a very good one, you may well feel unrelaxed in your own house. Most experienced nannies prefer to be in sole charge and do not like the feeling of being watched, however discreet you are.

It will help this situation if you:

- Divide areas of responsibility clearly.
- Leave your nanny in sole charge when you want to — enjoy it!
- Get out by yourself while you can.
- If it is your second baby, be flexible — your nanny already has a routine and daytime social life. Try and accommodate this within reason.

With a second or subsequent baby you will need to review her duties; it is also usual to increase her salary to reflect the extra responsibility and work.

Depending on the age gap, most children experience feelings of jealousy of their new brother or sister. Having a second loved person in the house can help alleviate this situation. Your nanny can work with you to prepare your first child for the arrival of the baby; when he/she is born, the nanny can look after the baby, allowing you time with the other child on your own.

If you are thinking of caring for a newborn baby be sure that you have the confidence and experience to do so. Your starting date will need to be agreed; if you are to be employed before the baby is born you will need to clarify with your employer what your duties will be. Be prepared to help the mother generally in that period.

Caring for a first baby has advantages:

- You can have a one-to-one relationship.
- You do not have to take over from another nanny.
- You are not tied to playgroup or school times.
- The baby is easily portable.
- Provided the baby is content you will have time to do your duties and have a break.

The disadvantages can be:

- You may find the job lonely or boring.
- It may be more difficult to meet people/other nannies.
- The parents of a first baby may be more protective, attentive and worried over him/her. You will have to be particularly tactful, patient and understanding.

Whether it is the first baby or not, it is likely that the mother will spend time at home with you and the children. If you are used to a sole charge job you may find this situation difficult. However, since it is only for a short while, you will have to adapt until the mother returns to work. Good communication with your employer is essential in this period; you will need to discuss:

- how to help the other children accept the new arrival and co-ordinate your approach.
- the routine and your duties while you are both at home.
- your terms and conditions.

YOUR OWN BABY: Some nannies are allowed to care for their own child at work. If you are able to do so you will need to consider your accommodation (if live-in), the compatability of the children and what you will do if your child is ill. If you become pregnant while working for a family and it is agreed you will stay with them after the birth of your child, you will have to be aware of what your charges may feel. Make sure you help prepare them in much the same way as if the baby were a brother or sister. After your baby is born and you return to work you will have to take extra care not to show any favouritism to any of the children and to be fair at all times.

See Also: First Nanny, Pregnancy, Type of Job

Penelope Leach, *Baby and Child* (Penguin).
A comprehensive practical handbook for the first five years of life.

Hugh Jolly, *Book of Child Care* (Sphere).
Comprehensive guide to child care.

Dr Christopher Green, *Babies* (Positive paperback).
A guide to surviving and enjoying baby's first year.

Peter Mayle, *Baby Taming* (Macmillan).
A humorous look at babies with practical hints and advice.

Janet and Allan Ahlberg, *The Baby's Catalogue* (Picture Puffins).

Helen Oxenbury, *Baby Board Books* (Walker Books).
Picture books on Dressing, Playing, Family, Friends, and Working.

Babysitting

Make it clear at the interview how much babysitting is included in the job and stick to that amount, perhaps even writing it into the contract. It is very easy to assume that the nanny will sit for you because she is there — this is not recognising her right to her own free time. If you want more babysitting than the specified amount, either give time off in lieu or be prepared to pay for it. Any nanny having to babysit unpaid four or five nights a week as part of the job is naturally going to be attracted to other jobs with shorter hours — although you may not find out until she hands in her notice that the hours were a problem, and possibly not even then. Long hours are one of the biggest drawbacks of a nanny's job and often a reason for moving on.

Always try to give reasonable notice of your babysitting requirements. It is unfair to announce at breakfast that you will not be home until two in the morning, and even worse to inform her through a scribbled note on the calendar.

Your nanny may want her boyfriend to come round when she

is babysitting. You need to decide how you feel about this; it is wise to have met him and indeed any friends who may drop in. If you do allow friends to visit, your nanny will be much happier to babysit but she should make sure your house rules are observed by her visitors.

Your nanny may be asked to babysit for someone else; if it is in her time off then it is her business, but if it means she

'Oh . . . you're back early. He's only just
started crying this SECOND'.

inconveniences you as a result or is tired during the day you need to discuss it with her. It is well worthwhile letting her babysit for others — she earns extra money, it gets her out of the house and it possibly earns you favours with others. However you should never offer your nanny's services to your friends without first consulting her.

Don't rely solely on your nanny for your babysitting; she may be ill or leave, or it may be her night off; at least one other person needs to be familiar with your household and available to help out.

Your nanny is a babysitter you can trust; if anyone else babysits for you it is essential that you either know them well or that they come to you with a recommendation. If you have an outside babysitter, always leave tea and coffee and food where necessary, full details of where everything is kept, and what to do if the children wake up. If your babysitter is familiar with drinks, favourite teddies and particular rituals she will find it easier to get the children back to bed and will know not to take any notice when they insist that 'Mummy always reads us all of *Charlie and the Chocolate Factory* before we go to sleep'. Always leave the telephone number and details of where you are going and a rough idea of when you expect to be back. If you are going to be later than expected, telephone and tell her.

BABYSITTING CIRCLE: This is an excellent idea – a group of you gets together and, paying with artificial currency (for example, tiddliwinks), you babysit for each other. Start a babysitting circle if one does not exist in your area, it is free and means you can avoid having to ask your nanny too often. You can of course have your nanny as part of the circle; using the same arrangement with her as you would if she was babysitting for you. Or she can be a paid member of the circle.

Quick Tip: Tell the children that you are going out, who will be looking after them and when you are coming back.

 The amount of babysitting you do will depend on the type of nanny job you have; as a live-in nanny you will be expected to do a given number of evenings as part of the job; as a live-out or temporary nanny, evenings are usually extra and paid by the hour. What will you be paid? Will you be needed at weekends? Will you babysit on the same evenings each week? The terms and conditions of babysitting must be discussed and agreed at the interview and not left vague – 'a few' could turn out to be five nights a week. If you are paid it will be at a babysitting rate; 'sitting' is often just that, although you may find yourself dealing with unforeseen situations, from a power cut to an ear infection.

Depending on how much free time you have in the evenings you may wish to babysit for other people. It is best to tell your employers if you are doing so. They should not mind how you spend your free time unless it is affecting your work the next morning. Usually nannies babysit for other nannies for free and for returned favours, but charge others by the hour. Make sure you charge people the same rate!

If you are going to be babysitting or having a babysitter, books are a good way to introduce children to the situation.

See Also: Contracts, Duties, Extra Children, Social Life

Shirley Hughes, *An Evening at Alfie's* (Bodley Head). What happens when the babysitter discovers water dripping through the ceiling.

R.O.S.P.A. *Guide to Good Practice in Babysitting*
Membership Dept,
Cannon House,
The Priory, Queensway,
Birmingham B4 6BS
Tel: 021 200 2461
A guide for parents and babysitters.

Banks/Building Societies

As a nanny you may find it difficult to get a credit card, loan or mortgage.

Unfortunately nannies do not score very highly on the list of points used by banks and building societies when they are considering whether or not to give an applicant credit. Some of these points are:

- Wage: a nanny's wage is low.
- Age: a nanny tends to be young.
- Number of jobs and length of time in each: a nanny obviously has a number of jobs, and is unlikely to be in any one for more than two years.
- Number of addresses over the past few years; a nanny changes address each time her job changes.
- Experience of managing money and paying bills; a nanny may well not have experience of this.

If you have an application rejected and you are creditworthy, you need not accept this as the final answer. The lender may not fully appreciate how a nanny's career is structured or the nature of the job. Arrange to have a face-to-face interview with the person who is dealing with your application so that you can ask why you have been turned down and argue your case.

At this interview:

- Wage: Explain how much money you have in hand at the end of each week. For example, the interviewer may not realise the perks of living-in — food, rent, light and heat all found — which leaves you with more in your hand than a young person on a low wage who has to pay for these things.
- Age: You will need to show that you are responsible, that even though you are young, you have a responsible job.
- Number of jobs: Explain that even though you may change jobs every two years or so, this is the nature of nannying and does not mean that you are irresponsible. Your change of address obviously relates to your change of job.
- Experience of managing money: be prepared to show them your recent bank statements and your payslips. You will need to convince them that you are responsible — a letter from your employer will help a great deal, and your general attitude is very important.

Quick Tip: Apply for your credit card/mortgage at the branch you bank at. You will have more chance of success if they know you and your bank account is consistently in credit.

See Also: Wages

Bathrooms

One of the biggest adjustments you have to make when you take on a nanny is no longer having the freedom of your own bathroom. Your relaxing bath can be transformed into a stressful unsatisfying splash by the rattling of the bathroom door handle every few minutes. The irritation which arises after half an hour of waiting to clean your teeth can explode into fury at the sight of a film of talcum powder over everything you need for that job. You may feel there is also something faintly unfair about the amount of time available to your nanny to primp and make up compared to your rushed three-minute ablutions, and this can lead to an uncharitable but very real resentment. You can help your nanny and your household to avoid bathroom battles by:

- Arranging times for each member of the household to use the bathroom according to their needs, particularly in the morning.
- Putting a lock on the bathroom door to avoid embarrassing meetings.
- Using it.
- Making it clear early on that you like the bathroom to be tidy, clean, with towels hung up and toothpaste removed from the handle of loo!
- If possible, giving your nanny a sink in her room, or her own shower room or bathroom which she perhaps shares with the children, or installing an extra loo/basin somewhere else in the house.

Your bathroom facilities will vary from job to job. Sometimes you will be offered a bathroom to yourself which is a bonus; more often than not you will share it with the children, which works well as you hardly ever need to use it when they do.

The most complicated situation is where the whole family shares the bathroom.

Do:

- Check the location of the bathroom when being shown around. Is it a quick run from your room and you are there or a Duke of Edinburgh Gold award hike to find it?
- Find out which side of the bathroom cabinet is yours, or will you have to take a packhorse with you every time you go to use the bathroom?
- Find out the procedure for use of the bathroom.
- Clean the bath after you or the children have used it — hopefully your employers will too.
- Keep your toiletries and any medicines safely out of reach of the children.

Don't:

- Spend too long in the bathroom if others are waiting.
- Use all your employers' expensive bubble bath.
- Rely on singing for privacy. Use the lock.

 Quick Tip: Plastic eggboxes, saucepans, sieves, squeezy bottles and yoghurt pots make good bath toys. Children can use them too!

See Also: Interviews, Privacy

Bedrooms

A good bedroom goes a long way towards making your nanny feel that you respect her and want her to be happy working for you — it is worth the effort and expense. If possible give your nanny a good-sized bedroom; if she is living in, it is her home, her bedsit and her place to entertain friends when you are at home and she wants to be private.

- Make it as comfortable as possible. Pictures, plants and a mirror all help.
- Give her a comfortable bed.
- Adequate heating is essential; she will spend a lot of time sitting around in her room.
- Give her a television and radio if possible, unless you are happy to listen to non-stop Radio One all day and watch *Neighbours* on TV every evening.
- Encourage her to make it her own and let her put what she wants on the walls.
- Don't go into your nanny's bedroom unless you are invited, unless you absolutely have to, or are worried about something. It invades her privacy and is unsettling. The state of it may also cause you unnecessary stress.
- Her room should be a child-free zone, and the children must be made to understand her need for privacy (once they are old enough). Having your work infringe on your free time is irritating; if *your* boss dropped in while you were watching television or talking to friends, however fond of him/her you were he/she would not be welcome!
- If you can avoid it do not use your nanny's room for anything else; if you have to, always arrange it with her beforehand.
- If you want your nanny to do night duty it is easier if she sleeps near the children's rooms.

Establish whether or not you want her to come into your bedroom to avoid any embarrassment or irritation.

It is important that you have a good look at the nanny's bedroom during the interview and decide whether or not you like it. It is the only part of the house where you will get any privacy and you will be spending a lot of time in it.

The location of your bedroom will make a difference to the amount of privacy you get. There are two extremes:

1. Quite apart from being embarrassing and occasionally entertaining, being in between the children's and the parents' bedrooms at the weekends can be like trying to have a quiet lie-in in the middle of Piccadilly Circus.
2. Having the east wing of the house to yourself sounds very grand and tempting but it can be very lonely and unnerving at times, if all other adults are in the west wing and your only company is a suit of armour.

Once you have moved into the room if you want to put up posters, pictures or shelves you will have to check with your employer that you can. Ask how they would like you to do so. If there is a cleaner find out whether or not she will be cleaning your room. If your room is cold, do not be afraid to ask for extra heating. Whether or not you let the children come into your room is totally up to you. When they are young it is hard for them to understand when you are on or off duty; but start as you mean to go on. Do not be afraid to gently send them back to Mum when you are off duty.

 Quick Tip: Respect and ignore your employers' bedroom.

See Also: Interviews, Privacy

 Dr Andrew and Penny Stanway, *Baby and Child Care Book* (Pan).
Section on beds, bedding and sharing.

Behaviour

Good relationships come from an attitude of tolerance, trust, flexibility, and a willingness to give and take and understand the other's point of view. Your behaviour is an indication of your attitude.

Living in close proximity with a stranger who is responsible for probably the most precious part of your life can cause enormous strain. The behaviour of all individuals involved is critical. The key is to be aware; both employer and nanny need to maintain a degree of detached professionalism in their relationships, within the limits of the natural attachment which forms as the weeks go by. Being a 'member of the family' and 'employee', or being a boss and a friend/mother figure, are difficult roles to play successfully; you can help your nanny by defining the role clearly and giving out strong signals as to which role is required at which moment. A clever nanny becomes adept at recognising the signals and adapting her behaviour to suit. A clever boss does not forget that even when she is offering advice as a friend, she is still the boss.

Never call your nanny 'my girl'. This is patronising, offensive and symptomatic of an attitude which causes conflict between nanny and employer.

If your nanny's behaviour changes it may be that there is something wrong which she is not telling you about and which you are probably unaware of. Have you changed *your* behaviour lately? Many employers do not even notice how their nanny is feeling, even less see the signals which are, however subtle, being given out. Look for signals; do not wait for the consequences of ignoring them to hit you in the face. This will help you to pre-empt crises and keep the relationship on an even keel. (You will not, however, be able to do much about the fact that her boyfriend did not phone her last night.) Draw a line between what is reasonable behaviour and what is taking advantage.

At all times your behaviour reflects how you feel about your job. You are working in someone else's home, in a very responsible job; bad behaviour reflects badly not only on you but on nannies in general. The media enjoys portraying stories of bad nannies and situations — you can help counteract this and improve the image of the profession by your good example.

When you are living and having your social life in your work place how you behave will make the difference between a happy job or one full of friction. Some families like their nanny to disappear to her room as soon as she goes off duty; others are more relaxed. Some are very friendly; others more formal. One of the most important skills to learn is how to adapt your behaviour to suit the family you are working for at the time.

CHILDREN'S BEHAVIOUR: It is essential that nanny and parents agree on the kind of behaviour expected of the children and co-ordinate their approach to the children's behaviour. Fighting, tantrums, teasing, clinginess, aggression, jealousy, manners, stealing, and whingeing are just some of the joys of child caring.

HANDING OVER: Be prepared for the child's change of behaviour once employer or nanny comes into the room. A child who has been behaving well for one person can turn into a monster when another arrives for many different reasons; he or she may be excited, relish the opportunity to create mayhem, want to be the centre of attention whilst the two adults are talking, or feel uncertain as to who is boss now that both carers are in the room at the same time. The situation overleaf is a classic example of avoidable conflict between nannies and parents in handling the behaviour of a child.

The nanny's authority has effectively been undermined, the child has learned that if mum comes in the rules change, and a dent has been made in the relationship between mum and nanny.

Always have a short handover period between you, and whatever rules have been set up, endorse them. The child cannot then manipulate either nanny or mother; he or she will see that the behaviour required by both of them is the same. The child also has time to adjust to whoever is taking charge. In this way both nanny and mother support each other and their authority is not undermined.

PROBLEMS: Since the nanny cares for the children most of the time she may be the first to notice adverse changes in their behaviour that may be cause for concern. Problems at school, illness or a change in routine — for example, the arrival of a new baby — can all unsettle a child.

Nannies have met with enormous resistance or even the sack on voicing their concerns for the behaviour of their charges. If a nanny is convinced that there is a problem then she has a responsibility to try to tell her employer.

It is vital that nanny and employer can communicate their worries and observations to each other about a child's change in behaviour without fear of upsetting each other. You need to establish and agree what has been happening, the possible cause and how you are going to deal with it. Having done this, both nanny and parents should talk to the child and, most importantly, liaise and co-ordinate their approach to his or her behaviour. If the difficult behaviour persists then the problem may be more severe and require professional help.

See Also: Child Development, Communication, Discipline, Guilt

---

Hiawyn Oram and Satoshi Kitamura, *Angry Arthur* (Puffin).
For five-year-olds. Arthur is frustrated and angry.

John Prater, *On Friday Something Funny Happened* (Bodley Head).
Two children are naughty all week until Friday, then they are good.

The major child-care books include sections on children's behaviour.

Bereavement

It is not within the scope of this book to tackle this subject in depth. We have confined ourselves to the basics as they affect the nanny, employer and children, and we have recommended books and organisations for those wishing for more help or information.

DEATH OF A CHILD: We all live with the hope that 'it will never happen to me' but, of course, it could.

Helen had sole charge of Joanna, who was two, an only child. She put her to bed for her midday nap and went downstairs to wash up. Joanna climbed out of her cot and fell down the stairs, fatally injuring herself. After a few days she died. Although Joanna's parents were very understanding, Helen's guilt was so great that she cannot now bring herself to look after children again.

Brenda was looking after an infant who suffered a cot death whilst in her care. The parents tried to sue her but she consulted a doctor and a lawyer who both advised her that there was no case to answer. Whilst Brenda lost her job she did not lose her livelihood and the reassurance she got from two professionals that she was not to blame helped her recover from what was a very unhappy and unpleasant time.

Deirdre's employers went away for a few days with their tiny baby. The baby suffered a cot death. Deirdre was utterly stunned when she got the phone call from the parents and offered to go and help them but she was not needed. Although she felt sad she also felt guilty — because she had hardly known the baby, and was not therefore very close to it, she did not feel its death as acutely as she felt she ought to. Although the family appeared to carry on as normal, the death hastened Deirdre's departure from that job.

If a child dies in your care and if your conscience is clear, try not to blame yourself. Feelings of guilt, depression, hopelessness, resentment, fear and anger are normal. Reactions to death vary enormously from family to family and person to person; every circumstance is different. At worst your employers may decide to sue you. This is where insurance is invaluable. Should this happen to you, if you are a member of a union it will be able to help you with legal aid.

If a child dies while in your nanny's care, you may feel that you do not want to employ her any more even if it was not her fault. Try and think clearly. Was she a good nanny and was this a genuine accident? Does she look after the children well? Would her departure create more problems than it would solve? She may not, of course, feel like staying with you, where she will constantly be reminded of the situation. You may feel the same about her. It may be wise to delay any immediate decisions. This is certainly a time to stop and talk to her, having thought it out from all points of view.

DEATH IN THE EMPLOYERS' FAMILY: If one of your employers' family dies, for example the grandmother, you will be leaned on for support and will need to help out a lot more than usual. Any offers of extra help/hours will be appreciated. You may need to be a good listener and offer a shoulder to cry on. You will need to use your intuition and discretion to know when to stay around and when to disappear. The parents will be caught up in arrangements and coping with their feelings, so your priority will be the children. They may be confused and frightened and need lots of reassurance; books can help you explain to them what has happened and help them come to terms with it. Do not be afraid to answer their questions truthfully, giving as much information as you feel they can cope with. If the family is religious, be sure to take account of their beliefs in your answers to the children. At some point you might help by taking them away for a few days to give the parents a break.

If you were planning to announce that you were leaving, it should be clear that now is not a good time. Look at the situation in the long term. Will staying on for another three months make that much difference to you? It will help the family and especially the children no end if you do.

 DEATH IN THE NANNY'S FAMILY: If you suffer a bereavement you will want to go home. Most employers will give you time off or perhaps friends can help you out. It is not just the first days of shock that you will have to cope with, but the days or even months after. Try not to take your emotions out on the children; it is not their fault.

Whilst there is no legal obligation to give compassionate leave, give your nanny as much time off as you can deal with if she is bereaved. If you cannot cope by calling on friends and neighbours, get a good temp and don't count the cost. A week's leave is reasonable, but you may consider giving her more in particularly difficult circumstances. Give as much support as you are able to when she returns, and explain to the children what has happened if they are old enough to understand.

See Also: Insurance, Leaving, Questions, Unions

Penelope Leach, *The Parents' A-Z* (Penguin).
Section on death.

Jacquelynn Luben, *Cot Death* (Thorsons).
Advice on coping with Sudden Death Syndrome.

Susan Varley, *Badger's Parting Gifts* (Picture Lions).
For four-year-olds and over. Badger's gifts help his friends come to terms with his death.

Jill Krementz, *How it Feels When a Parent Dies* (Gollancz).
For seven-year-olds and over.

Which, *What to Do When Someone Dies* (Consumers Association/Hodder and Stoughton).

CRUSE,
Cruse House,
126 Sheen Road,
Richmond, Surrey TW9 1UR
Tel: 081 940 4818
Offers practical advice and counselling for the widowed
and their children.

League of Compassionate Friends,
6 Denmark Street,
Bristol, BS1 5DQ
Tel: 0272 292778
Offers support to bereaved parents.

Foundation for the Study of Infant Deaths,
35 Belgrave Square,
London SW1X 8PS
Tel: 071 235 1721
Offers support to bereaved parents whose children have
died suddenly and unexpectedly between the ages of
one week and two years.

Some hospitals offer counselling services for the
bereaved.

Boyfriends

You suffer the unfinished ironing, the burned saucepans and the hours in the bathroom. You imagine a
vision of Tom Cruise dimensions. When you finally
meet the cause of all the chaos you cannot take your eyes off his
spots. What was all the fuss about? Boyfriends can be a source
of humour, help and happiness or the curse of your life; they can
turn your nanny against you, burn holes in your furniture and
eat you out of house and home without a thank you. They can
be surly and dismissive, viewing you as an inconvenience to be
ignored, or pleasant and agreeable, great with the children and

good at mending broken toys. Their effect on your nanny is total; they are ignored at your peril. You will need to strike a balance between locking them out and giving them the key to the drinks cabinet.

Boyfriends and children rarely mix successfully during working hours, and there are many horror stories ranging from the children being threatened by a jealous boyfriend to children witnessing torrid scenes in front of the fire. However, boyfriends are an essential part of your nanny's life. It will help if you remember what it felt like yourself. Some employers are very restrictive, others more liberal; whatever your attitude, the reality is that a nanny will be happier if her boyfriend is allowed some access. How much will depend on you, her attitude, and whether you like and trust her boyfriend. If you do, make him feel welcome. Whatever the situation, house rules regarding boyfriends must be clear and firm and should be respected by the boyfriend as well as the nanny.

Although you may not want to, you can find yourself in the role of mother with regard to your nanny and her boyfriends. Many employers feel that their nanny is worthy of a 'better' boyfriend; be very wary of passing comments on your nanny's boyfriend since by so doing you are criticising your nanny over something which probably matters more than anything else to her, and your concern may well be misinterpreted. If her relationship with her boyfriend is making her moody and affecting her ability to handle her work — tackle the moods, not the boyfriend.

Finding and keeping a boyfriend while nannying is not always that easy. A nanny's boyfriend has to be very long-suffering; he must be patient and enjoy children since he is going to hear a lot about them. Boyfriends have been known to leave nannies in search of girlfriends who can make the cinema for seven o'clock and who won't embarrass them with baby seats and nappies in the back of the car.

'I know the invite said "Bring a bottle" but REALLY . . .'

Once you have met Mr Right or even Mr Wrong there are certain do's and don'ts to be aware of.

Do:
- Tell your employer if you have a boyfriend and introduce him at the first appropriate opportunity.
- Find out what the rules are with regard to boyfriends.
- Make it clear to him that you have to adhere to the house rules and that he must respect them too. A boyfriend constantly calling in during the day will soon be found out.
- Children have big eyes, ears and mouths. Nothing engenders distrust in your employer more than the feeling that you are putting your boyfriend before the children.
- Try to keep your emotions away from your job. It is not always easy, especially when you feel like walking on air or burying yourself.
- Make sure your boyfriend understands that it is not his place to discipline or take charge of the children.
- Be careful what information you give a new boyfriend to

start with; bear in mind the safety of the children and the house.

Pam met Stuart in the park. She dated him for a week and then explained she would not be able to see him for two weeks as she was going away with the family. When they returned from holiday the stereo, video, microwave and jewellery had gone — and so, too, had Stuart.

– Consider your employers' feelings before asking if your boyfriend can stay the night. Whilst some have a very liberal attitude, others may allow it but may not want him to share your bed. Some may be concerned about the example being set to their children; others may have objections on religious grounds.
   Think about these things before asking.

Don't:
   – Take a job in an area you would otherwise not choose just because your boyfriend lives there.
   – Make hasty decisions with regard to leaving a job because you have ended a relationship. Your feelings/the situation may have changed a week or two later.
   – Introduce the children to too many boyfriends. It can be very confusing and unsettling for them to see a constant change.
   – Get involved with one of your employers' friends or relatives — this more often than not leads to complications and conflict and can turn out badly for both sides.

One nanny was beginning to think she would never have a boyfriend. She had her eye on the bloke who worked in the local garage. He did not seem to notice her since she was always covered in baby goo or holding hands with a five-year-old. So she decided to take decisive action. On a T-shirt she had a message that he could not miss printed across her chest. It read 'THESE ARE NOT MINE'.

'I think she means the kids . . .'

See Also: **Privacy, Social Life**

Breakages

Breakages can be a major source of irritation, depend-ing on the attitude of the nanny. If she is honest, apologises and is generally concerned about the break-age you are more inclined to forgive her. If she hides it, pretends it has not happened or that it is nothing to do with her and hopes that you will not notice it, it is annoying; and when it happens more than once it is infuriating.

A nanny may not be aware of what something means to you since she is unlikely to have a house of her own and may only have ever lived in her parents' house, where she may take things for granted. If you have anything that you particularly care about, tell your nanny. Do not expect her to live in an antique shop while looking after two young children. She is probably in the house for more hours than you while the children are up and about, and therefore breakages are statistically more likely to happen to her. You may feel that she is being paid to look after the children and that therefore she should not have accidents, but accidents are usually just that.

- Put anything precious or valuable out of the way or out of reach while children are young.
- Cover your possessions for accidental breakage through your contents insurance, making sure your nanny is covered too.

One of the worst things that can happen to you when you have just started a job is to break something. You do not know what is precious or what has been broken three times before; you may spend all day walking around feeling sick because you have broken a vase, only to be told by the mother later that she is glad it is broken because she hated it. This however is preferable to discovering that that dirty old plate, which is now in pieces in the dustbin, was priceless.

However careful you are, the inevitable will happen. Just when you think all is well and your charge is happily playing with the lego while you hang the washing out he is actually scribbling on the walls, tearing up cassette tapes and smashing the crockery. If something gets broken:

- Do not avoid the issue; it will not go away. Hiding the broken object will make things worse when it is finally discovered.

- Take responsibility, be honest and apologise.
- If it is mendable, keep the pieces.
- Do not ring your employers at work. It is better to wait until they come home and then explain what happened.
- You may want to offer to pay for the broken object. Hopefully household items, including yours, will be covered by your employers' contents insurance.

It can be embarrassing if something of yours gets broken when you are not there. Try and keep things that really matter to you out of reach. If something does get broken and it is important to you show your employers and discuss it with them.

See Also: Household Maintenance, Insurance

Callers

 Since few callers call at the weekend it usually falls to the nanny to deal with them. She should have a list of likely callers and always be told when someone specific is expected. An awareness of the potential dangers of callers, both wanted and unwanted, is essential and it is a good idea to talk about guidelines for dealing with them:

- Discuss a clear line of rejection with her: for example, she may want to say, 'I am not the householder and cannot buy anything or make appointments on behalf of the owners.'
- Be sure you are happy for your nanny to sign for completion of any work done, for example, carpet laying. In so doing you are giving her the responsibility for agreeing that the work is acceptable.
- Give her payment and a letter of authorisation if needed.

People will try and sell you anything from old iron to religion.

- Do not let unauthorised callers into the house. It is better to offend a bona fide caller than to give an unwanted caller access.
- Never leave the children alone with a caller.
- Do not tell a caller, either on the phone or at the door, the movements of the household.
- If in doubt about a caller or his work, check with your employer as soon as possible.
- Ask to see identification cards where appropriate, for example, meter readers.

See also: Safety

Cars

Most nannying jobs involve some use of a car. You may work for an employer who provides an appropriate car which is serviced regularly; you may work for an employer who gives you the Mercedes while she drives to her top executive job in the Mini; or there is the employer who gives you the 'S' registration Fiesta ('good little car that') and is completely surprised when anything goes wrong with it — while her Saab goes into the garage for the slightest squeak. Whatever the car, you need to be aware of the following:

SAFETY: Before driving your employer's car it is vital to check with her that it is insured for you and has tax, MOT and the correct safety equipment. Ask to be shown the routes to school, playgroup, hospital, garage, town and anywhere else you may need to go.

Never put the children into the car of another driver who does not have suitable seat belts, since ultimately this is your responsibility.

USAGE: Find out exactly what use you will have of the car. Will you be able to use it just for work journeys or in your time off too? Some jobs offer a car that you share with your employers. Establish how this will work out to avoid disappointment and friction later on.

If you are going to be using your own car in the job discuss and agree the terms and conditions. Contact your insurance company and explain the new situation; they will tell you if any extra premium is due. If so, your employer should reimburse you for it and also provide adequate safety equipment. You will need to agree what proportion of your maintenance bill will be met by your employer. She will want to see your tax and insurance certificate.

PETROL: Your petrol allowance needs to be organised. Every family does this in a different way. Any petrol used for your job should be covered by this allowance, but make sure you are fair about putting petrol back in if you have taken the car out for your own use.

You may find that your employer asks you to do extra journeys but then does not offer any more petrol allowance. If you are in the situation where the allowance is not covering the mileage, explain why you need more, ideally when asked to do the extra journeys. It will help you if you keep a record of your mileage for a week or two.

MAINTENANCE: Your employers will appreciate it if you keep the car clean inside and out. Car washing makes a good activity for the children too! Check the oil, water, air in the tyres, and the windscreen washer water from time to time. You are helping yourself in the long run.

 Quick Tip: A towel under the children's seats saves the covers from unsavoury delights.

BREAKDOWNS: Most nannies dread anything going wrong with the car as they feel guilty about it and irritated by the inconvenience it is going to cause. Most employers will be reasonable when you tell them but some make you feel as if you did it on purpose, or that you are imagining it. Whatever you think their reaction will be, it is important to tell them if you think something is wrong with the car, no matter how difficult it may seem; then you are covered should anything further go wrong. If you do break down, keep the children with you.

 Quick Tip: Jump leads connect black to black, red to red. Connect the black leads first.

A car is a substantial part of the expense of employing a nanny and is one of the perks which make a job attractive. Primarily a car is there to enable your nanny to take your children where they have to go but if you can offer her the perk of having it for her own use as well, do so. It also pays to provide a reasonable car if you can afford it — when a nanny is choosing between two jobs, the car may make all the difference.

Do:

- Make absolutely sure your policy covers your nanny; this may increase the cost since she may well be under twenty-five.
- Check her driving licence.
- Ensure that the car is equipped with the correct safety equipment for the ages of your children and any others who may ride in it.
- Make sure your nanny uses the safety equipment.
- Make sure she never leaves the children alone in the car, particularly if they are old enough to get out of it.
- Provide an adequate petrol allowance and pay it regularly.
- Clearly establish what you will and will not pay for early on, including parking fines.
- Make sure she understands the basics of how the car works, for example, oil, water, battery top-up.
- Service the car regularly; breakdowns with children are frightening and can be dangerous.
- Talk through the procedures in case of a breakdown; you may want to give her AA membership or similar.
- Ask her to report any faults to you immediately she is aware of them, however small these may be. It can be annoying to use the car one weekend only to discover that the clutch is slipping and the handle has fallen off the nearside door, and that you have not been told.
- Keep a spare set of keys where you can both find them.

Don't:

- Expect the milometer to stay the same.
- Expect the car to run on hot air.
- Expect the car to stay in pristine condition.
- Allow her to pick up hitchhikers.
- Allow her to lend the car to anyone else.
- Give her the 'reliable' old banger.

 ACCIDENTS: It is every nanny's nightmare to have a car accident with children in the car. The following notes may help:

IN THE EVENT OF AN ACCIDENT

- Reassure and stay with the children.
- Make them and the car as safe as possible.
- Look for a witness and take name, address and phone number.
- Take the other driver's name, address, home and work telephone number, and insurance policy details.
- Note the make, colour and registration number of the car.
- Note the time, place, weather conditions, road markings, car positions.
- Note what you think happened.
- Note the policeman's number.
- Note the garage address and number if the car is taken to a garage.
- Write anything else down you think may help; you may forget later and shock may prevent you thinking clearly.

You will be asked all these questions later on and you will feel much better if you can answer some of them.

 Quick Tip: Keep pen and paper in the car.

As soon as possible contact the parents. Whilst informing them will not be easy, try to tell them as calmly as possible. Give them as much information and reassurance as you can.

If the outcome is serious your employers will want to discuss your job situation with you. You may feel you cannot work for the family any more. At the very worst your employers may bring legal action against you. Contact a solicitor; your local Citizens' Advice Bureau can help or your union if you are a member.

You may well find that your confidence in your nanny evaporates if she has an accident with the children in the car, even if no one was badly hurt. Support her as much as you can and help restore her confidence. If you feel you cannot trust her any longer you have no option but to ask her to leave.

> *Sue was involved in a car accident with the children in the car. No one was seriously hurt but the car was a write-off. The parents were very understanding and kind. She wished they would be angry and tell her that what she had done was unforgivable, because that is how she felt. She wanted to buy them flowers, but they gave her some. When life got back to normal she put off leaving for six months because she felt guilty and did not want to add to the family's problems.*

See also: Accidents, Cost, Insurance, Safety, Schools

Looking After Your Car. Reader's Digest Basic Guide, includes a breakdown guide.

Child Abuse

Child abuse takes different forms, both emotional and physical, and includes verbal abuse, threats, violence, neglect, cruelty and sexual abuse.

Nannies are at the front line in this area and as such bear a lot of responsibility. Most nannies are completely trustworthy but unfortunately the press highlights the horror stories, putting fear into every employer's heart and sickening other nannies who put care, love and attention into their jobs.

Be absolutely clear about how you want your nanny to discipline the children, particularly in relation to smacking, and be sure to be consistent in your approach. Agree on your rules, co-ordinate this with her, and discuss it frequently. When the children suffer cuts and bruises in the normal course of their daily lives, ask your nanny to tell you what happened each time for your own peace of mind.

Abuse from a nanny is most likely to be in the form of verbal abuse, cruelty or smacking. If you are in a position of having to dismiss your nanny for suspected abuse, you will need to inform the agency, if you used one, and since you will want to protect other children she may look after, you will obviously not provide her with a reference. Whilst you may decide to report her if you are convinced of abuse, be aware of the serious consequences of doing so for all concerned, particularly the children.

If you suspect child abuse, either by your employers or their friends or relatives, or by another nanny, you are in a very difficult situation. If you speak up you may, depending on the circumstances, lose your job, and you will have set in motion a train of events which will be very distressing for the child, the family and yourself. Reporting child abuse can result in the splitting up of the family and the children being taken into care. However, if you keep silent the child may continue to suffer, and you have to live with your conscience, even if you do decide to leave. Therefore before you act it is essential to be convinced that your suspicions are correct. If so, contact your local health visitor or social services department; the NSPCC will also give advice and help.

Quick Tip: Explain the children's cuts and bruises to your employer as they occur.

There is a strong argument for the establishment of a register for anyone working as a nanny in a private house, in the same way that one already exists for childminders. The NNEB have recently established a Principles of Professional Practice document, which is the beginnings of a register of nursery nurses.

Both nannies and their employers can help protect children from abuse by teaching them self-worth and self-respect; by talking to them about their rights; by letting them know that they can talk to you about anything that is worrying them, and by making it clear that they will be believed and taken seriously. There are several books for adults and children which cover this subject very well.

See also: Discipline, Leaving

 David Pithers and Sarah Greene, *We Can Say No* (Beaver Books).
For ages three to seven. A guide which helps prepare children for dangerous situations.

Michele Elliott, *Keeping Safe* (Bedford Square).
Has a large section on child abuse and talking with children about it.

Sherryll Kerns Kraizer, *The Safe Child Book* (Futura).
How to protect the child, prevention against child abuse including strangers, school and relatives.

National Society for the Prevention of Cruelty to Children,
67 Saffron Hill,
London EC1 8RS
Freephone: 0800 18188
Tel: 071 404 4447. 24-hour response.

Parents Anonymous,
6 Manor Gardens, London N7.
Tel: 071 263 8918
A self-help group set up to help parents who are afraid
they may abuse their children. Can also help with other
crises too.

Childline
Freephone: 0800 1111. 24-hour response.
Tel: 071 239 1000.
Enquiries, normal office hours.

Child Development

One of the reasons many mothers give up work is so that they can watch, monitor and shape the development of their children. Your children's development and progress can be a source of pleasure or worry; the first time your child smiles, writes his or her name, or rides a bike without stabilisers, are moments of great joy. To miss out on these moments can make you feel guilty and unhappy. A good nanny can help alleviate this.

If you are interested in your child's progress ask her to tell you what the child has done during the day. Make time for regular discussions and encourage your nanny by showing her that you appreciate her efforts.

If a nanny is trained and experienced she will have a good knowledge of child development and, since she will probably spend more time with your child in the company of other children than you do, she is in a good position to assess the child's progress or spot any possible problems should they arise.

Situations have arisen where nannies have been sacked when they have voiced their worries over a child's development; make it clear early on that you welcome your nanny's observations and opinions even if you do not agree with them.

As the children's nanny you are in a prime position to develop the potential of the children in your care. This includes the development of physical, intellectual, social and creative ability, language skills and emotional stability. It is important to understand the various stages of development; there are many books on this subject to help you.

As important as a knowledge of child development is, what matters most is the right attitude to the child — being prepared to talk, sing, laugh, dance, play games, draw and paint, read and create stories, explain, share and, most important of all, be interested in the child's world and what he or she thinks and says about it.

Parents are constantly concerned about the development of their children and look to you for progress reports and to tell them if you are worried about anything. Report the good and the bad. All employers enjoy being told of their child's achievements. Some may ask you to keep a daily diary. You will inspire confidence and trust if you show them that you are aware of the child's needs and you are interested in his or her development.

The doctor and/or health visitor offer developmental checks at six, eight and eighteen months; then at five and eleven years. Do not wait for these if you are worried about something; discuss your concerns with your employer and agree who should take the child to the clinic to see the health visitor. If you are the one to take the child to the clinic, be sure to report back to your employer on the child's progress.

See Also: Activities, Behaviour, Communication

Penelope Leach, *Baby and Child* (Penguin).
Comprehensive guide to development.

Richard Woolfson, *Understanding Your Child* (Faber and Faber).
A guide to understanding child development including advice on how to cope with common problems.

Hugh Jolly, *Book of Child Care* (Sphere).
Covers all areas of development.

Mary Sheridan, *Children's Developmental Progress* (NFER).
A guide to all stages of development from birth to five years.

Clothes

Taking care of the children's clothes is part of nursery duties; this includes washing, ironing and sewing.

– A routine is essential. A well-ordered wardrobe and a system that leaves all the children's clothes cared for makes life easier.

– If you are asked to sort out the children's old clothes, be tactful if they are around. They are often sensitive about their belongings.

– Ideas on what a nanny should wear to work vary from uniforms to tracksuits; discuss this at the interview. Either way, clothes need to be practical and comfortable since children take a huge toll on them.

– If you are a live-out nanny it is a good idea to leave a change of clothes for yourself at the house in case of accidents.

When your nanny first joins you, give her specific instructions about the care of the family's clothes. What exactly is she responsible for, and is she expected to both wash and iron the clothes?

– Explain fully how the washing machine, tumble-dryer and iron work before leaving her on her own to use them. This minimises the number of pink shirts and shrunken jumpers.

- If you have any articles of clothing that need special care (for example, wool or silk) tell your nanny how you want them washed. Access to a chart of washing symbols is a good idea.
- If you ask her to buy clothes for the children, make sure you explain exactly what you want.

 Quick Tip: Measure the children's feet frequently — shoe shops do not mind if you do just that.

See also: Duties, Shopping

 Shirley Hughes, *Alfie's Feet* (Bodley Head).
Alfie gets new boots and has problems with his left and right.

Pat Hutchins, *You'll Soon Grow Into Them, Titch* (Bodley Head).
Titch is upset at oversized hand-me-downs, until he goes shopping and passes some of his clothes on to the baby.

Barty Phillips, *The Complete Book of Cleaning* (Piatkus).
Advice on all aspects of cleaning, and information on cleaning products and equipment.

Communication

'My boss is always late home and never apologises.'

'She never gives me my money on time — I always have to ask for it.'

'I can't plan my social life — I never know when she's coming home.'

'The telephone bill is enormous.'

'She never gives the children fresh home-cooked food, it's always out of a tin, even when I specify.'

'Her boyfriend is more important than her job and the children are suffering.'

These are classic moans, all of which might be solved or reduced by good communication.

Good communication between you and your employer is vital; you will have a happier job if you are working for someone you can relate to.

First impressions are very important; during the first telephone call you make in answer to the advert, consider whether or not you can talk to the employer easily and whether or not they listen to you. Keep this in mind when you go for the interview.

Once in your job make an active effort to communicate. You will need to talk to your employers about the day's events and the progress of the children, and you will find that many problems can be avoided simply by talking about them as soon as they come up. Your employers will not realise that you are not happy about something unless you tell them: do not rely on subtle hints — they may be missed by a busy employer.

Be aware that your employers may also find it hard to confront you with a problem. When they do, and providing their comments are fair, treat them positively and act accordingly. Hopefully you will not have to deal with continuous unfair criticism.

If you do not discuss problems with your employer they may well get bigger, making you frustrated and angry. The end result of this may be that you consider leaving a job that you were otherwise happy in. Good communication reduces problems. However, 'talking to your employer' requires courage and time — both of which may be in short supply.

Daily events and future plans are best dealt with at a set time, for example during the evening meal (although establishing and keeping to a regular set time is not always easy).

If you need to discuss something difficult with your employer, for example, wages, tax, or leaving, think carefully about what you want to say and how you are going to say it. Then, if possible, choose a time when the children are not around. It will also help if you have thought about what you would like the outcome of the discussion to be and how you think the problem you are discussing could be solved. You may prefer to talk to one parent at a time about these matters, usually the mother since she is most often the one who employs you.

Confronting difficult issues is never pleasant. If you have decided that your complaint is not unreasonable, take a deep breath and put your case politely but firmly. Do not give up — you can be assertive without being unpleasant, and it is not wrong to stand up for yourself. You may not solve the problem the first time round but you will have laid the ground for future discussion.

Nanny: Can we clarify my hours once more?

Employer: They haven't changed.

Nanny: Well, no, they haven't changed officially but unfortunately you have been late home four nights in a row this week and I have worked around seven hours more than we agreed.

Employer: (Embarrassed.) Oh. Well I did say my hours weren't always predictable.

Nanny: Yes, but we agreed I could have time off in lieu.

Employer: Well I can't do that for a bit.

Nanny: My friends all finish at 7 pm and I can't plan my evenings if I don't have a definite finishing time.

Employer: Let me try and sort something out.

Nanny: That would be great if you could. Thank you.

The nanny has opened up the discussion about hours and if things do not improve, she can return to it, knowing that the onus is on her employer to sort the situation out.

Sometimes I wonder if we have a slight communication problem....

Communicating with your nanny is not always easy: physically, since you are usually out when she is in and vice versa; and emotionally, since you do not have the structures of a work place to support either of you. Also, the central issue is a burning one — your children.

It is easy to say 'talk to each other', but in practice it is not always easy to talk about things when the employee/employer line is constantly confused due to the unique employment situation. You may find it hard to be the boss in your own home when the nature of the work is your children. It may be easier to be the boss in a structured environment where the pecking order and relationships are usually clear and formally defined through salary, size and position of office, closeness to the boss, and so on, and where you may well have the support of colleagues.

Good communication requires courage and effort; as the employer you are anxious not to appear critical but you will be annoyed if things are not being done as you would wish. You either bottle things up and explode over something small and unrelated to the main problem, or simmer with resentment and sour the atmosphere; alternatively you may say nothing and despise yourself for being weak/walked over/taken advantage of. Either way, the more unspoken niggles you amass the terser your tone of voice when dealing with your nanny, leaving her perhaps wondering what is wrong and you irritated and disheartened that things are not improving on their own. They don't!

Your nanny will know when she is not doing things as well as she should be; if you do not communicate clearly to her that you are aware of it she will continue to do so and the balance of power will become unhealthy. A lot of us avoid speaking up for fear the nanny will leave; however, not dealing with things can leave you coming home late to avoid talking to your nanny, and there may be a general heavy atmosphere in your home which eventually affects you, your partner and your children. If things are really bad, she is probably best elsewhere but you can only help the situation by airing the problem. Decide what is and is not important; you will never have everything exactly as you want it and it is probably best to compromise with the minor irritations and tackle the major ones.

For easier communication:
 1. Let your nanny know at the start that you realise there are always problems when people are living and working closely together and that you expect her to raise them with you and to be open to you raising them with her.

Make it clear that these problems relate to all aspects of her living and working with you, not just the children. Often the most difficult problems to address are those little things which involve you and your nanny, for example, coming home to find the fridge empty and the ham you had intended for supper used for the children's tea.

2. Be sure to allow time regularly for discussion of problems. If your nanny knows you will listen to her in an unhurried way at least once a fortnight, and give thought to what she is saying, you stand a better chance of being able to confront and solve issues than you do if she has to fight for ten minutes of your time just as you are leaving and the children are demanding her attention.

3. Do not avoid discussing something which keeps occurring if it is bothering you; your resentment will increase every time it happens and the longer it goes on the less you will feel able to keep it in proportion and deal with it calmly.

4. Think how you can express what you have to say in a positive fashion, and try to avoid heavy criticism. Communicate your approval as well as your disapproval. For example, 'I really appreciate the way you keep the children's rooms in order — could you do the same for the kitchen after you have used it?'

5. Watch for unspoken signals and, without becoming paranoid, see whether you have done something recently which is causing them. For example, in an otherwise cheerful nanny, sulkiness or avoidance when you come in late in the evening may mean that you have done it once too often without explanation or apology.

6. State your expectations clearly, firmly and directly. Do not expect hints to be understood. For example, rather than 'You seem to be seeing your boyfriend rather a lot lately' say 'Can I remind you of our house rule regarding boyfriends — I do not expect them to visit during the day except when you are off duty.'

7. Be wary of tackling all the problems in one sitting. If you

do, she may feel severely criticised and react badly to your concerns. If possible deal with each thing as it occurs.

8. Offer a solution to the problem if possible.
9. Do not give up. Be assertive but pleasant. Many of us find being employers in our own homes a hard thing to do; it can make us feel guilty. This does not help the situation however, and you have a right to ask for what you want, provided it is reasonable, and expect to get it.

If a problem cannot be solved by good communication, and you continue to be upset by it, it is time to objectively review the situation. Many employers continue a relationship which has long since passed its sell-by date 'for the sake of the children'; in the long run this is counterproductive.

NOTES: You may find you spend a lot of time writing notes asking your nanny to do things; notes can be misconstrued and the message in them may seem more intense than it actually is. Whilst notes are a good idea for keeping each other up to date on a daily basis, never use them to communicate something really important or delicate.

Employer: I'd like to talk to you about sweets. I realise that you give the children sweets after school.
Nanny: Yes I do — we go into the shop and all their friends get sweets so it's very hard not to buy them too.
Employer: Yes, I appreciate that it is difficult — do you have to go in the shop?
Nanny: Well, I have to get the milk from the shop for you.
Employer: Could you get the milk on the way to school rather than afterwards?
Nanny: There isn't always time before school.
Employer: Well, perhaps you could go beforehand where possible — I really would like you to limit the amount of sweets they have.
Nanny: I'll try.
Employer: Thank you. I appreciate that.

You have offered the nanny alternatives, making her aware that you know what is happening and that you are not happy about it.

Gael Lindenfield, *Assert Yourself* (Thorsons).
How to be assertive, including techniques.

Beverley Hare, *Be Assertive* (Optima).
Explains how to express yourself, giving example conversations.

Confidentiality

A live-in nanny is in a unique situation, living at her work place, and is therefore privy to confidential information which would not normally be available to her in another job.

Be professional in your approach to confidential information, for example divorce, moving house, pregnancy, illness, financial and other family matters. If you sign a contract there is usually a clause requiring you to respect your employers' confidentiality. You can be dismissed if you breach this contract.

It is important to maintain the right distance between you and your employee if you are to keep your authority in the situation. It will help if you keep the amount of personal and confidential information available to your nanny to a minimum; this removes any possible temptation she may have to gossip, keeps the balance of power healthy and gives you a greater feeling of security.

See also: Contracts, Privacy

Contracts

Contracts are required by law: under the Employment Protection (Consolidated) Act 1978. After thirteen weeks an employer must give her employee a 'statement of employment'; this can be in the form of a letter or a formal contract supported by a side letter.

Whilst it has not been common practice in the past for employers to formally contract their nannies, both employers and nannies are now using contracts more and more. Apart from being useful as a reference for negotiation in a dispute, they make both sides focus clearly on what they are offering and getting.

Employers can be guilty of thinking that the nanny will do anything and everything, and nannies can imagine that once they are in the job it will not matter if they do not do some of the things which were discussed at the interview. A contract helps avoid this; it also helps make both sides feel more secure.

The Federation of Recruitment and Employment Services issue a standard contract which can be obtained from them if you write enclosing an s.a.e. The FRES contract is used by some agencies, and training colleges; it is also recommended by *Nursery World*. PANN also has a standard contract which can be used; or you may prefer to draw up your own.

If you are going to draw up your own contract, be sure to include the following points:

- Name and address of employer.
- Name and address of employee.
- Job title.
- Starting date and expected period of employment.
- Trial period: if you feel that this is necessary/practical.
- Notice period: normally four weeks on either side after one month.
- Salary: how and when paid, arrangements for tax and National Insurance contributions, and review. If only part of the nanny's salary is to be declared for tax purposes, that amount only should appear on the contract. The rest can be agreed as expenses in a side letter.

- Main duties, i.e. nursery only/sole charge. Specific duties can go in the side letter.
- Hours: including time off and babysitting where this is part of the agreed number of hours.
- Holidays: number of weeks, public holidays, when taken, holiday pay entitlement.
- Sick pay: including arrangements for sick pay, sick leave.
- Pensions: Employers rarely provide a pension. It is a legal requirement to state that there is no pension.
- Sackable offences: include both those which will result in instant dismissal, those which will result in a warning and if not heeded, dismissal, and disciplinary and grievance procedures.

Signed (Employer)_____ Signed (Employee)_____

Date:_____

This contract covers the basics. Since no two nannying jobs are ever the same it is also important to have a letter covering the particular terms and conditions of the job, as it is the minor details which are frequently the major source of friction.

It is a good idea to include the following in a side letter:

- Duties: nursery, household, animals.
- Extra babysitting: amount, notice, payment.
- House rules: friends, boyfriends, smoking, telephone.
- Car: usage, petrol.
- Expenses: amount, what for, when paid.
- Accommodation: self-contained, shared bathroom.
- Overtime or additional payments if any.
- Availability for travel.

 Quick Tip: Update the contract when the terms and conditions change.

A contract will not help you:

- If a nanny is set on leaving without notice. She is better left to do so. If she has decided to go immediately you will not want to keep her in case she takes it out on the children. You are unlikely to sue and she knows this.
- If an employer is set on dismissing a nanny without notice. The nanny has no option but to go without a fuss; however, if she feels she has been unfairly dismissed and she is a member of a union she can ask them to take up her case.

Dear Deb,

Enclosed is your contract. Just to clarify the little details:

1. We will require you to travel with us on our annual holidays to Cornwall but agree that we will honour your prebooked skiing holiday in February, Safari to Kenya at Easter and Caribbean trip in July.

2. You will be required to babysit for two regular nights a week, Mondays and Thursdays, apart from the weeks when I am filming and then it is Tuesdays and Wednesdays, apart from the weeks when my boss is drunk, and then it is Fridays and Saturdays. If I have no meetings and the trains are on time and my husband is not clamped it will be Mondays and Fridays, unless we are away when it will be every night anyway.

3. Our house rules are no boyfriends in the house after 10.30 pm and no smoking. This includes out of the bedroom window and in the porch when it's raining.

4. As agreed you can have total use of the car. The jump leads, tow rope and blanket are in the boot. Petrol will be covered by expenses on the condition that you give us the tokens.

5. Please use the baked beans, telephone, hot water and lights economically.

The children look forward to meeting you — sorry they were out last Thursday.

Yours,

Mikki Take

See also: **Babysitting, Duties, Holidays, Hours, Illness, Interviews, Leaving, Wages**

Costs/Expenses

It can be disheartening to work hard, see your children seldom, and have nothing left in cash terms to show for your efforts. Since most of your salary can go on the nanny's wages you may tend to block out the additional costs and avoid focussing on them except when you absolutely have to, i.e. when the nanny asks for more money. And then you are always amazed that the ten-pound note you gave her two weeks ago was not made of elastic.

When you take on a nanny for the first time you are probably not fully aware of how greatly she is going to affect your outgoings; it is useful to be aware of the actual extra costs involved.

COSTS WHICH A NANNY BRINGS:
- Wages, tax and insurance.
- Car if relevant, petrol, insurance, repairs, maintenance, depreciation.
- Food for nanny and her nanny visitors.
- Telephone calls. These include those the nanny makes on her own behalf, as well as the children's.
- Light and heat. The house is in use twenty-four hours a day, instead of the few hours that you spent in it before and after work before the children were born. This adds substantially to your light and heat bills.

Alison came home late with a nanny friend and was drinking coffee in the sitting-room when the door opened and in walked the cost-conscious father stark naked; he had not heard them come home and had come down to turn out the light. On seeing Alison and her friend he panicked and ran in the wrong direction to the kitchen, leaving himself no way out. He grabbed the oven gloves and arranged them to cover his embarrassment, beating a crab-like retreat out of the door.

- Insurance: possible extra premium to cover accident and injury.
- Furnishing her accommodation. You may need to buy a second television, install a hand basin or shower, and generally make what was a spare room into a comfortable and appealing bedsitter.
- Outings: nannies undoubtedly take children out more than you would yourself, since they are at work whereas you — if you were there — are in your own home and therefore probably happier to stay in and work on your own projects around the house with the children alongside you.
- Bonuses, gifts, rises.

If you budget realistically from the beginning for the extra cost that having children and a nanny is going to bring, you will cope with it better as it arises.

EXPENSES:

Your nanny may imagine that your pockets are bottomless since you are older, have a good job, own a house and a car, and go abroad for holidays; she may therefore think that the odd ten pounds here and there is unimportant. Since expenses have a habit of expanding to use up the cash available, it is a good idea to have a fixed amount in mind and ask her to stick to it if possible.

You may choose to give her a regular amount each week for expenses or you may prefer to pay as you go along. Either way it is a good idea to have some system of accounting; this rules out any possible suspicion of dishonesty, shows you where your money is going and shows your nanny that you are concerned about the wise use of your cash.

Expenses may cover:
- Petrol. Often separate from other expenses.
- Food. Weekly shop or extras only.
- Shopping. Household items running out, child care goods too.
- Outings and school trips and entertainment.

- Treats. Lollies, ices or toys.
- Household. Collecting dry cleaning, shoes, posting letters.
- Children's clothes and shoes.
- Presents for other children.
- Fees for group activities.

Expenses can be the bane of a nanny's life; constantly being asked to buy things for the children or for your employer but not being given any money to buy them with, (which at worst can leave you without enough money for yourself) can get very wearing. You can avoid having to subsidise your employer by discussing expenses thoroughly early on in the job and establishing a method of payment which works for both of you. You may have to try several different methods before you find the right one.

Your employer may not be fully aware of what you are spending money on. Do not be afraid to speak up for more money if you legitimately need it. Where possible always ask your employer before you overspend the set amount or buy something expensive.

Never use your employers' money for yourself unless this has been agreed.

Expenses can be paid in a number of ways including:

- Being given cash as and when asked for.
- Being given a set amount of cash on the same day each week. More only for special needs.
- Having a kitty which is topped up with cash when the employer sees fit or when the money runs out.
- Keeping a record of expenses, and then being paid back weekly or monthly.
- Using a credit card for the family's expenses only and the employer paying the bill.

Whatever the method used it is advisable to keep some sort of record, even if you are not asked to. This will make both you and your employer feel more comfortable. Keep receipts if you think the amount will be questioned or the goods will need to be changed.

➡ Quick Tip: Use a separate purse or wallet for your work expenses.

See also: Cars, Telephone, Tax and National Insurance

Curriculum Vitae

A c.v. looks impressive, shows you have thought about presenting yourself in the best possible light, and gives prospective employers something concrete to keep when you leave the interview. An employer is not just looking for your professional details, she is also interested in what sort of person you are, which your c.v. should tell her.

Your c.v. should include:

- Title, name, surname.
- Address, telephone number (with code).
- Date of birth.
- Nationality.
- State of health.
- Education (secondary onwards) and qualifications.
- Employment history (dates and type of job).
- Additional skills.
- Hobbies and interests.
- Referees and their telephone numbers.

Whilst you may not need a c.v. if you apply for jobs through an agency, it can be useful to have a record of your experience and it is a good idea to keep it up to date just in case you should need it.

A c.v. can be a useful reference after the interview to remind you of the nanny's details once she has gone and before you have made up your mind; it also gives you something to write on during the interview and is a talking point if you need one. However, a nanny who offers you a c.v. is in the minority.

Detective's Guide to CVs

I have experience with children.　　I have looked after the next door neighbour's/my best friend's children once or twice.
My hobbies are fashion and music.　　I spend all my money on clothes and play loud rock music.
I have looked after all ages of children and have gained a lot of experience.　　I am a restless person who moves on frequently.
I love animals.　　If I don't have to clean them out.
I love meeting people.　　I am looking for a good boyfriend.
I like to travel.　　But not with children.
I can cook basic meals.　　If you provide the tin opener.
I like reading.　　*Chat* and *Bella*.
I prefer sole charge.　　I can't read my paper if you are looking over my shoulder.

See also: Advertisements, Interviews

Discipline

You will want to agree and co-ordinate your approach to discipline with your nanny, particularly in relation to daily life, for example, food, eating, nappies, potty training, sibling rivalry, language, television, manners, relationship to other children, and other age-related problems like temper tantrums, biting and bullying.

Consistency is very important if you are not to undermine the child's security and give out confusing signals, therefore encouraging him or her to play you and your nanny off against each other. It is no good instructing your nanny not to buy sweets and then hitting the sweet shop for a quiet life when the weekend comes — your nanny is then faced with 'Mummy lets us' during the week and, at the moment of discipline, may not know whether Mummy does or does not. She will also lose heart if her efforts to carry out your wishes are not backed up by your actions.

It will increase your child's sense of security if you both use the same rules and apply them more or less in the same way. If you cannot agree on a way of handling a problem, ultimately your nanny must do things your way — you are left with the end product!

It is essential to decide what form 'punishment' takes in your household and discuss this fully with your nanny, making it clear that, provided she sticks to your agreed methods, you support her fully. If, for example, you use withdrawal of privileges as a punishment, your nanny may well have to carry this out on your behalf (for example, no television) and vice versa. Make sure therefore that what you set up is realistic and that you are not making a rod for your own and your nanny's back.

Since they are not her children your nanny will undoubtedly find disciplining them easier than you do; she is not struggling with guilt, tiredness and the general strains of being a working mother and will probably therefore give in less easily than you will!

You will never be able to be absolutely sure that your nanny is disciplining your children as you would wish; coming home early unannounced or having the neighbours keep an eye out are often used as ways of checking up on your nanny; however, these are not always reliable. Trust your instincts and watch and listen to your children.

Discipline is almost always brought up at your job interview; if it is not, you should bring it up since it is central to your job. You need to establish your employers' views on and methods of discipline since if your way of disciplining children is very different from theirs you will find it very hard to handle the job. It is important to be able to agree and exercise the same discipline as your employers; back each other up, as this gives the child less room to manipulate you both.

Discipline will vary from family to family and you will learn to adapt. What one family regards as acceptable behaviour another may not, especially in the areas of manners, social behaviour and language. During the first few weeks of working in your new job you will be able to learn exactly how the parents discipline the children by watching and listening to them as they deal with the situations that arise.

You will find it useful to regularly discuss and sometimes review the children's discipline with the parents, both when it is causing you difficulties and when it is working. If you have to severely discipline a child, be sure to tell the parents exactly what happened. This is preferably done when the children are not around, but on occasions it is good for the children to see that you talk to their parents about them, and that their parents endorse your actions.

Monday:	You agree with your employer that, before watching TV, your eight-year-old charge will tidy his room.
Tuesday:	Having failed to persuade the child to tidy his room you ban the TV and cope with a two-hour sulk.
Wednesday:	You try again; after twenty minutes of argument the child's bedroom is tidy and he watches TV.
Thursday:	This time you do it in ten minutes.
Friday:	The penny has dropped. To your delight you find that the child has tidied his bedroom without being asked before watching TV.
Saturday:	Your day off. You get up to find the child watching television and his bedroom in a shambles. You stick your head in the oven.

The above situation, or one like it, will probably unfortunately be familiar to most nannies. Nothing is more defeating than being asked to carry out some form of discipline, only to see it not carried through by your employer. If this does happen to you, whilst it is obviously irritating, it is probably not serious enough to make an issue out of; remember that your employer is not working when she is with her children — it is her privilege to break the rules, even though this may cause you problems. As a professional nanny you are paid to do as you are asked and you will just have to live with it. If, however, you are asked to enforce the discipline which has just been undermined, in the future you could tactfully ask your employer to help you by backing you up.

SMACKING: This is one of the most controversial areas of discipline, and it is not within the scope of this book to go into it in depth. There are many books written by child-care experts which include useful sections on the subject. Whilst 'never smack' is excellent advice, there are few adults who care for children who can honestly say that they never have smacked a child. As with all other forms of discipline, smacking needs to be discussed honestly and fully by mother and nanny at the interview.

See also: Behaviour, Child Abuse, Communication

 All the major child-care experts have large sections on discipline in their books.

Divorce

If there are serious marital problems in the family you are working for it will be a very difficult time for everyone. You may end up unwittingly being piggy in the middle, desperately trying not to get involved. Your priority will be the children, who may well turn to you for stability. It is important that you carry on with your duties and keep the children's routine as normal as possible.

A divorce will affect the behaviour of the children, who may feel rejected, depressed, guilty, worried and unhappy. You can help by listening to them and trying to answer their questions where possible. Since the parents will not be their usual selves during this time it may be very difficult for you to communicate with them; even so, find an appropriate moment to ask them how they want you to answer the children's questions. There are several books written for children on this subject which may help you and them.

The lead-up to a divorce is not easy for a nanny; keep out of the way as much as possible, try not to take sides though you may probably like one partner more than the other; and avoid ending up as go-between — this is not your job. If the situation gets really nasty you could offer to take the children away for a short while.

When appropriate you will need to find out how your job will be affected in the long term when the parents have separated.

If you were planning to leave before the divorce was announced it is obviously now not a good time. This is one of those situations where if it does not make too much difference to you, staying a little while longer will be very helpful, particularly to the children who will not then have to cope with another big change in their lives at a very insecure time.

A nanny, if she is prepared to stay through the divorce period, provides stability for the children when the two most important people in their lives are having a difficult time. If you are lucky she will stay with you and remain with the partner who has the children, although this new situation will obviously need discussing, since it is presumably not the one she came to in the first place.

Once you have established a new pattern to the life of your family, you should consider reviewing your nanny's terms and conditions, since they may well have changed along with your lifestyle.

- Will you still need a full-time nanny?
- Which of you will have custody of the children?
- What are the guidelines for custody?
- Will she be taking on any more children?
- Will she be expected to go and stay with your ex-partner with the children?

Whilst your financial situation may not be easy, it is a good idea to offer her some more money or time off if you are able to and want to encourage her to stay. Apart from the emotional strain, she will inevitably have to take on a bit more work to compensate for the lack of the other partner, and may also be faced with extra children to look after.

If you are divorced from the children's father when you take on a nanny, discuss this with her. She will need to know how to handle the situation, particularly in relation to any custody arrangements you have. If the situation is a difficult one she should be given clear guidelines for dealing with it. A great burden of responsibility can be placed on the nanny — she should not be put in the position of go-between or mediator. Be sure that she is mature and capable enough to cope with any problems, if there are any, before taking her on.

See also: One-Parent Families, Questions, Stepchildren

 William Arnold, *When Your Parents Divorce* (Westminster).
For older children.

Beth Goff, *Where is Daddy?* (Harper and Row).
For younger children.

Rosemary Wells, *Helping Children Cope with Divorce* (Sheldon Press).
Deals with telling the children, living in two homes, step-parents.

Angela Williams, *Divorce and Separation* (Sheldon Press).
Guide for women with practical advice.

The Divorce Conciliation and Advisory Service,
238 Ebury Street,
London SW1 0LU
Tel: 071 730 2422
Send a sae for information and book list.

National Council for the Divorced and Separated,
13 High Street,
Little Shelford,
Cambridgeshire CB2 5ES
Tel: 0206389 6206.

Doctors

When you start your job, find out:

- The children's medical history, including injections, illnesses, treatments and allergies.
- Any relevant family medical history.
- Where the medical cards/health records are kept.
- Who the family doctor/dentist is and where the surgeries are held.
- When the next doctor's/dentist's appointment is and whether you will be required to take the children.

Be prepared:
- Encourage regular health and dental care at home.
- When you keep an appointment, talk about where you are going and why.
- Read stories on going to the doctor/dentist.

– If possible visit the surgery first with the children.
– Make a note of emergency numbers.
– Play doctors/nurses and dentists. Making or improvising a first-aid kit can be fun.
– Do 'doctor', 'dentist' jigsaws and fuzzy felts.

Go to the doctor if:
– Your employer asks you to go, regardless of how you feel about it.
– If *you* think the child needs a doctor. Ask first if possible, but do not wait for permission if you are worried about the child's condition, for example, high temperature or prolonged symptoms.

Take:
– Mother's note if you want it/need to for back up.
– Supplies (e.g. nappies, drinks) and distractions.

Afterwards:
– Arrange next appointment.
– Write down what you were told and what you told him.
– Telephone one of the parents if convenient/necessary.
– Get prescription.
– Praise and reassure the child.

 Quick Tip: Tell the doctor/dentist that you are the nanny.

If you need to go to the doctor/dentist yourself discuss the best time for this with your employer; it is not unreasonable to have time to do this but you can help minimise the inconvenience by fitting it round the routine of the family and children. You do not need to explain the reason for your visit unless you wish to.

Whilst you may prefer to take your children to the doctor or dentist yourself, you do not want to start taking time off work for the smaller things and risk being seen as inefficient in organising your home life.

A nanny can be as good as you at taking the child to the doctor/dentist — she is more detached and therefore calmer, particularly when it comes to things like immunisation. Make sure she knows the child's medical history and what you want her to ask the doctor — she cannot help the doctor if she does not.

Curtain Up

'Hello. I wonder if you can help me? I'd like to make an appointment for Luke Jackson, please.'

'Sorry, Mrs Jackson, we can't fit you in for an appointment but if you'd like to come along at 11 o'clock, we'll see what we can do.'

'I'm not Mrs Jackson . . .'

Once at the surgery, true to form we push the pull door and pull the push door into the waiting room. Having finally got inside and joined the queue of people without appointments, I turn round and face what is to be our audience for the next hour or more, all sitting neatly in quiet rows. Oh God!! No other children!! It's better if there are — there's a chance that they might be less well behaved than yours. Mainly middle-aged men. They don't understand children. And old dears. I hope they are deaf. I sit down trying to look cool, calm and collected. Huh. I can cope. Luke senses the silence so starts to sing at the top of his voice, louder and louder. I let him, so he then turns to me and says 'I shouting!!'

'Yes.' I tell him nicely. 'You are.'

He gets down. Luke is going to surpass himself and show off and I will end up being the cabaret. Here he goes, up to the front, checks out that people are watching and then starts. He does a head over heels, then claps, followed by running in a circle flapping his arms, then falls over superbly and bumps his head. Enter Angee stage left, who carries him back to his seat muttering suitable caring words.

Half an hour gone. Can't be much longer. Time for a drink. Out comes child's beaker, orange juice, and abracadabra, this will impress, scissors! I cut the corner of the carton and pour the juice into the beaker, giving it to Luke without spilling a drop. He then proceeds to shake it everywhere like a salt mill.

Three quarters of an hour later, the audience is thinning out a bit. I feel like selling popcorn to the rest. Luke decides he is in need of some more exercise. Rifling through the free leaflets, he selects one on contraception and, after a quick look, hands it to the nearest old dear.

Red-faced and to various looks of amusement and disgust, I decide it is time to let them know I am not his mother. It may help on the sympathy scale. 'Come on, Luke — be a good boy — then we can tell Mummy how good you were. Mummy's at work, Daddy's at work. Angee's looking after you. That's right.'

We have the place to ourselves. Luke takes the opportunity to have a rest and settles down with a book. Typical. I tidy up the debris.

Buzz. Buzz. 'Mrs Jackson . . .' But I'm not . . . Oh never mind. We finally go in. Ten minutes later we leave, all sorted out with an 'It's OK' and a pat on the back. We pass the receptionist. 'Good afternoon, Mrs Jackson.' I laugh to myself. We push the pull door and pull the push door and tumble out into the empty car park.

See also: Illness

Dr David Delvin, *Common Childhood Illnesses* (Corgi).

Brian Ward, *Life Guides Dental Care* (Franklin Watts).
A factual book for the older child.

Gurilla Wolde, *Emma and the Doctor* (Hodder and Stoughton).
For under fives.

Anne Civardi and Stephen Cartwight *Going to the Dentist* (Usborne).
For three years upwards.

Jill Coleman, *Simon Goes to the Optician* (A&C Black).
Simon gets some glasses.

Duties

Your duties will vary according to the type of job you
take (nanny, mother's help, au pair) and the circumstances of the family you work for. The advert may
briefly mention the type of duties involved, for example,
'Nursery duties only' or 'Light housework' or 'Muck in'.

Before you follow up the advert it is a good idea to decide
what duties you are ideally prepared to do. Once you get to the
interview and find out more about the job you may feel
prepared to take on duties that you would not normally consider
if there are other things about the job that you really like.

It is generally agreed that nannies' duties include:

- CHILDREN'S CLOTHES, BEDDING AND TOWELS: This
  includes regularly washing, ironing, sorting out and
  putting away items; sewing and carrying out the repairs
  needed; and generally making sure that school uniform is
  marked and clean. The children's shoes also need to be
  looked after.
- CARE OF THE CHILDREN'S BEDROOMS, BATHROOMS,
  PLAYROOMS: Regularly making them clean, tidy and
  generally taking care of the equipment in these rooms.
- GENERAL CARE OF THE ROOMS USED DURING THE DAY:
  For example the kitchen, sitting-room or dining-room. At
  the end of the day anything you or the children have used
  or made should be cleared up and the rooms left as you
  would like to find them.
- COOKING FOR THE CHILDREN: Providing them with a
  balanced diet suitable for their age.
- LOOKING AFTER THE CHILDREN'S HEALTH, HYGIENE,

DEVELOPMENT, SAFETY: This is a very wide and varying area ranging from nail cutting and hair washing to reading and teaching road safety.

- PROVIDING PLAY, EDUCATION AND EXPERIENCES: Suitable to the age of the children in your care.
- TAKING AND COLLECTING FROM SCHOOL/PLAYGROUPS/ AFTER SCHOOL ACTIVITIES: Making sure the children have what they need to attend and are there on time.
- BEING AVAILABLE TO BABYSIT THE AGREED NUMBER OF TIMES.
- CARING FOR THE CHILDREN'S BOOKS, TOYS AND WORK: Including cleaning, repairing, and keeping the parts together. Displaying the children's craft work, drawings and photographs in appropriate places.
- CARING FOR YOUR OWN WASHING, IRONING, COOKING AND ROOMS.

As well as the above, some jobs will involve some of the following duties which will need discussing and clarifying:

- NIGHT DUTIES: If the children wake in the night, how many nights are you expected to attend to them?
- WEEKEND WORK: How often are you required to work weekends and will you be given days off instead?
- HOUSEWORK/CLEANING: Are you expected to do any extra household duties, other than those specified above? If so, what are they? Try and avoid vague descriptions like 'just muck in and lend a hand' — you will not be able to argue later when you find this means doing all the housework.
- GENERAL SHOPPING: Does this mean every so often or doing the weekly household shopping for the whole family?
- CARE OF PETS: This very much depends on the type of pets kept. Are they totally your responsibility or would you just be required to help out?
- CARE OF PARENTS' CLOTHES: Are you expected to wash, iron and sew these or just some of these jobs?

– COOKING FOR THE WHOLE FAMILY: How many meals does this include and how often?

Once discussed and agreed, your duties should be written into a contract or side letter. You then have a starting point, should problems arise.

Many problems occur over household chores that are difficult to define as duties but are more to do with living in a family and helping each other; for example emptying the kitchen bin, bringing in the milk bottles, or cleaning the grillpan.

Both employer and nanny are not really sure who should do what and both have a good reason for avoiding the chore! Hopefully, you will all share the job without saying anything about it. However, you may fear that if you do something once you will have to keep on doing it, so what starts off as helping out can end up as just another of your duties, which can make you feel put upon. If this happens, be assertive and ask to discuss the problems and clarify just what your duties are.

At some stage you will be asked by your employers to do them a favour, which may be anything from collecting the dry cleaning to changing your day off at short notice. Where possible and provided you are not then taken for granted, it is a good idea to do these favours as they will build up a feeling of goodwill with your employer. It also makes it much easier for you to ask for a favour in return, (for example extra time off or having a friend to stay) and establishes a good relationship of give and take.

As with all jobs, once your initial enthusiasm has gone some duties can become very boring. Be sure to keep up all the duties you agreed to take on; setting yourself standards to meet and having a routine will help. Not keeping up with your duties will be a major source of friction between you and your employer.

It is essential to define exactly what you want your nanny to do at the interview, and consolidate this in the first few days of her working for you. It will be more difficult to introduce duties later on once she has got into a routine. It is not the duties which are easily defined and written down that can cause upset — it is the myriad of little things which occur on a daily basis. Employers often assume that nannies will do the things they would do if they were at home; whilst nannies obviously vary according to their personality and upbringing, most will not — either because it is not their home (it is their place of work); or, if fully trained, they will often only want to do the duties they were trained to do.

One of employers' main gripes is that their nannies start off in a job doing everything well and once the initial enthusiasm has waned, their standards slip. Any relationship between your family and a nanny has a natural life; there will come a moment when you will start to notice that things aren't being done as well as they might be or as enthusiastically as they were in the first few weeks. Whilst it is not easy to redress this successfully once it has happened, there are a few guidelines that may help put that moment off:

- Treat her as a professional and make it clear that you expect professional standards.
- Define her duties at the beginning, and reassess these periodically with her once you have established a routine.
- Be realistic about your nanny, taking into account her age, personality and experience; you will inevitably have to compromise, so do not expect her to be good at everything, and decide which areas are important and which matter less.
- Thank her where appropriate. This cannot be stressed enough, particularly if she has made an extra effort (for example, a child's birthday party) or done something extra to help which is not strictly part of her job (for example, got the bedroom ready for granny who is coming to stay that evening). We all like to feel appreciated, and since most nannies are often still in their teens, they in particular need encouragement and praise and a visible acknowledgement of their efforts. A nanny who works for weeks on end and whose employer hardly seems to notice what she is doing or how will not have any incentive to do that bit extra.

- Deal with those duties which are not being done immediately, before they become a grey area.
- If you do have to confront her with things she is not doing, do it politely and firmly but be sure to give her a chance to put her point of view and listen to it. If she puts things right, be sure to notice and thank her for doing so. This will help repair any bad feeling which may have arisen as a result of the confrontation. If she does not put things right it is time to start looking for a new nanny.
- Make sure she establishes a routine which fits around the family; this makes overseeing her duties that much easier.
- Make sure you are not asking her frequently to do more than you agreed, or if you are, that you are aware of it. If you gradually start adding new duties to her week she may well compensate in other areas without telling you, particularly if you take these for granted. It is important for both sides to be aware of the balance and not take any situation for granted. For example, if you give her Monday afternoon off two weeks running, be aware that she may think she is entitled to it thereafter; if she feeds the horses two Friday evenings in a row you may assume that she is going to do that from now on.

See also: Babysitting, Contracts, Hours, Interviews, Pets, Routine, Shopping, Toys, Type of Job

Extra Children

These are children you look after either regularly or occasionally, for payment or as a favour, for friends and neighbours, in addition to your regular nanny job. Before embarking on caring for extra children, ask yourself:

Are the children's ages compatible? (Although it can help if they are, it does not necessarily matter if their ages are different, depending on the children and how many you have.)
– Does it fit in with the daily routine?
– Do you have enough equipment and space?
– Are you confident you can cope and happy to do so?

GET PERMISSION: Always ask your employer before agreeing to help out with other people's children — she has a right to say no. (She may feel that her own child will be neglected, that she is already paying you to do a job for her, or that she does not like the other child/mother/family.)

AGREE TERMS: Before agreeing to take on an extra child, discuss it with the extra child's mother/nanny: you will need to talk about hours, frequency, what you will be doing and where, whether or not you will be going out in the car, and payment. The going rate is usually based on the local childminding hourly rate. If you are going to be paid, be sure that either you or the child's mother have cleared the arrangement with your employer.

Once you have the go-ahead make sure you know about any particular problems the child may have and that you have the parents' work telephone number and telephone number of local friend/neighbour.

After you have looked after the extra child for the first time, report back to both sets of parents. A full report reassures them that it was a good thing to do and makes it easier for you to look after extra children again.

Your nanny may be given the opportunity to look after extra children. It can be a bonus:

- She earns more money which makes her happier.
- Your child has company (provided the age is right and the children get on) and has the opportunity to learn social skills, like sharing.
- Your nanny becomes part of the nanny network, makes friends and combats loneliness.
- You are doing another mother a favour indirectly and making contacts which can be useful for sickness/holidays/ emergencies.

You need to be sure that:

- If your nanny is to be paid the other mother has cleared this with you, either directly or through your nanny.
- You agree with your nanny the hours she will be taking extra children on.
- You or the other mother provides the correct equipment (for example, car seats) to ensure total safety for both children.
- The other mother/your nanny accepts that your nanny is only available if your children are not sick, need to go to the doctor, etc.
- You know where your nanny will be with the children.
- Your child enjoys the company of the visiting child and that their ages are compatible where relevant.

You may want your nanny to take on extra children — perhaps those of a friend or relative in the holidays or in an emergency. However, never offer her services to another without first talking it through with her to make sure that she has the confidence to cope with those extra children.

If you do ask her to take on extra children, make sure that, if you did not make it clear at the interview, you consider giving her more money or perks for the period of extra responsibility. Be prepared for the possibility of her having to drop some of her customary duties to cope with the new workload.

See also: Stepchildren, Type of Job

Fathers

The father may figure a great deal in your job and take an active part in the children's lives or he may very rarely be around and may not affect you at all. Sometimes the father will be at your interview. Find out what he does for a job and how he will fit into the routine. If he is not at the interview try to meet him before you start work where possible – you will need to feel that you can live and work with him too.

If the father takes an active part in the children's lives, he may well be the one to give you instructions and offer help when needed. Make sure you involve him in what is going on so that you do not cause any misunderstandings between him/the mother and yourself.

Some fathers work from home; if this is the case you will need to come to agreements over how much he will participate in the day, when and if he is to be disturbed, and generally how this will affect your routine.

The following are problems which sometimes arise with fathers:

- Giving you instructions which conflict with those of the mother. If so, tell him and agree whose instructions you are to follow.
- Undermining your authority.
- Asking you to do extra duties.
- Making advances.
- Being unfriendly. If this is extreme you might want to discuss it with the mother but you will need to tread carefully since you will obviously not want to offend her.

On the other hand, you may have the advantage in some households of the father being your ally and helping you with misunderstandings and problems with the children's mother.

Fathers can be a bane or a boon; the Dad who is well housetrained, who helps look after the children at weekends and who is aware of the slog of keeping several children occupied, safe, fed and watered day in day out will support you and your nanny. He will help you sort out the difficult moments, probably be more detached and lend a feel of impartiality in any dispute; he may act as comforter, friend and comic relief to you both. He may, if you are lucky, be aware of and appreciate the effort you put in to making a good relationship with your nanny.

The father who is rarely there, does not see much of his children, has a horror of the nappy bin and no desire to involve himself in playdoh or puke is of less use to you and of no use whatsoever to your nanny; he may not understand what all the fuss is about when she forgets to buy the wetwipes or leaves the children's wardrobe empty on a Friday evening because her boyfriend failed to phone the night before and he will not want to deal with the inconvenience if it affects him.

If you are married to this sort of father, you will be on your own when it comes to dealing with your nanny's misdemeanours. He may even undermine your carefully established rules and upset your routines. If this is the case, make it clear to your nanny that you are the boss and that all decisions come through you. If he does upset her he must be stopped and made to realise how important she is to your sanity.

Discuss and agree the terms and conditions that your nanny is to work under with your partner and make sure you back each other up in dealing with day-to-day problems and events. This avoids putting your nanny in the situation of having to deal with two separate sets of instructions. You will also need to clarify who she should go to for her wages and expenses.

Remember that it is intimidating for a nanny to have to negotiate with two employers at once; if things are particularly difficult, your husband might restate your case separately. However, avoid the temptation to delegate the difficult problems to your husband — this will not do anything for your nanny's respect for you.

Be wary of leaving the father out or worse, of siding with nanny against him; this is not fair to her or to him.

See also: Advances, Communication, Duties

 Tony Bradman, *The Essential Father* (Unwin).
A guide to becoming a dad.

Jan Ormerod, *Dad's Back* (Walker).
For under-fives.

First Job

Before starting your first job it is a good idea to give yourself a few days to make arrangements, get organised and, if possible, have a break. The following tips may help:

PACKING: Try and ignore the urge to pack your entire record collection, your exercise bike and cheese plant. In the first instance, take enough clothes to cover all eventualities and a few things to make you feel at home. After you have been there a few weeks you will know what else you need and can bring it back with you the next time you go home.

BOOKS: It can be reassuring to take some books with you for reference, books with advice on child care, development and psychology, first aid, creative play, activities, cooking for children, and maps and guides to the area if you have them. Take a few children's books with you if you have any — showing the children 'your' books is one way of helping to build a relationship with them.

WATCH CHILDREN'S TELEVISION: Making yourself familiar with current TV programmes can also help you form a relationship with the children: for example, if you have learned at the interview that they have a particular favourite, showing them that you know a bit about it will give you a starting point for conversation.

GET UP TO DATE WITH YOUR HEALTH: Visit the dentist, doctor, family planning clinic, and so on.

GIVE FAMILY AND FRIENDS YOUR NEW ADDRESS: Ask people to write to you. You are bound to feel lonely the first few weeks and receiving letters helps a great deal.

ARRIVE THE DAY BEFORE: at a time which suits your employer. This will give you time to settle in before you start work.

In the first few days, you may feel awkward while the parents are around, not knowing where anything is, where you should be, what to say and how far you should go with looking after and disciplining the children. Use your common sense and initiative, pick up guidelines from the way the family behaves with each other, and ask lots of questions. You will have found out a lot about the family and the children at the interview, but you will still need to clarify the following points:

- What the children are and are not allowed to do.
- The children's likes and dislikes.
- Any special family slang, nicknames, (for example, names for private parts and bodily functions).
- The children's social lives and activities.
- The routes to the school, doctor and hospital.
- How the washing machine, dishwasher and other appliances work.
- How to work the heating system, and when you should do so.
- Addresses and phone numbers of children's friends' parents, clubs, groups, dentist, doctor, garage, grandparents, house, neighbours, other nannies, parents' work, police, playgroup/school, vet.

Do not put off getting this information together as things can go wrong even on the very first day.

A trip to the park was in order for the first afternoon in my first job. Tim, aged five, persuaded me to take everything bar the kitchen sink as his 'last nanny had always let him'. We set off complete with picnic and sister Sarah in her pram. We had not been there long when Tim needed to go to the toilet. I sent him into the bushes. He emerged screaming: it appeared he had caught his willy in the zip of his shorts. With the aid of some passers by I managed to call an ambulance. Once at the local hospital I had trouble answering any questions. Family doctor? Child's date of birth? Any allergies? Parents' place of work? It was lucky that Tim knew enough to help me; his mother was contacted and gave permission for the anaesthetic which allowed the doctors to free him. After that, I made sure that I had all the information I would ever need.

'Well, if you don't know his family doctor or his date of birth, perhaps you could at least tell me the poor child's NAME'.

BEING ACCEPTED: One of the most difficult things in the early days can be getting the children to accept you; they are probably missing their old nanny and may well push you to find out what your limits are. They may reject you initially or they may compare you to their old nanny and insist that she let them do things which you are not happy about. If this happens and you are not sure how to deal with it, check with your employer. Do not be disheartened; be consistent and you will gradually establish your authority and routine.

Jobs often start with a trial period of anything up to three months. This gives you and your employer a formal basis on which to end the arrangement if you feel that the job is not for you, and makes it easier to do so.

Your first job is very important as it will influence the way you feel about subsequent jobs. Some potentially good nannies give up after their first job, if it was an unhappy one, when, had they made a move early on, they might have found the right job for them.

There are both advantages and disadvantages associated with employing a first-time nanny. Nannies vary enormously according to their age, disposition, experience and character; whilst some mothers think that an experienced nanny is essential at all costs, others are looking for a type of person first and experience second. Much depends on the age, sex and number of your children, and whether or not you are to give her sole charge.

If this is your nanny's first job:

- She will not compare your household and children with any others she has worked for and therefore, provided that you are reasonable, will probably be more prepared to do what you want her to do in the way you would like her to do it than a nanny whose third job it is.
- You will be setting the standard for her future jobs.
- She may be more enthusiastic with the children and keen to please you.
- She will not have developed any bad habits/short cuts.
- She will be less expensive than an experienced nanny.

However:
- She will be new to the situation of working/living in the same place and inexperienced in coping with problems which may arise either with you or with the children.
- She will not have the wisdom and perception of an older and more experienced nanny and, depending on her maturity, may find controlling older children difficult.
- She may not have much practical experience of all the things she learned in theory on her training course and therefore have to learn as she goes along.
- She may need more guidance and help with establishing

routines and finding her feet.
- She will probably be very young and may either hang around you and your husband when off duty or be out every night with a different boyfriend.
- You may feel as though you have taken on a daughter not an employee.
- She will probably only just have passed her driving test.

See also: Household Maintenance, Overlapping, Previous Nanny, Social Life, Training

---

First Nanny

You may have an image in your head of the reliable, cheerful, kind, efficient, loving nanny who will take over and run your family selflessly and with no thought to her own life; a cross between a slave and a housekeeper with boundless energy and a capacity for self-sacrifice reminiscent of imperial India. These nannies disappeared with the Raj and fortunately today's nanny, like most women, wants to get something out of the job for herself.

The following list of dos and don'ts apply to all nannies, not just the first, but are particularly relevant to your first nanny:

Do:
- Talk to other people who have nannies and if possible, talk to the nannies themselves.
- Write down her terms and conditions either in contract form or in a letter of agreement.
- Have periods when you are at home with her and your child.
- Establish lines of communication on the first day and continue to work at your relationship with your nanny.
- Set standards clearly and, whilst not being overfussy, ensure that they are met.

- Write out a list of things which will help her in her first few days.
- Introduce her to some of the neighbours, friends and any other nannies there may be working locally.
- Ring her occasionally to see if she is coping — but don't overdo this, too many phone calls can unsettle her.
- Be aware when you have a good nanny and make an effort to keep her. So many employers only realise how good their nanny is once she has left.

Don't:
- Expect her to have the same attitude to your child as you do. She is trained to work with children; you gave birth to them and they are yours. Like as not she has no children of her own.
- Expect her to have the same standards and values as you; her background, education, family, friends are unlikely to be the same as yours — she may therefore find things which you take for granted quaint or unnecessary.
- Assume she will do things your way — show her, in relation to *your* child and to *your* house and household.
- Hesitate to deal immediately with serious or sackable offences.
- Worry that the child will get more attached to the nanny than to you. Children always know who their mothers are, and — except in unusual circumstances — given the choice, choose their mothers. If you are employing a nanny, you must be prepared to share the child with her — jealousy is counterproductive. Be glad if your child is attached to her. Children who have had nannies have the benefit of learning to rely on more than one adult, which may help them when they have to adapt to life outside the home, for example at playgroup or school.
- Be vague about those awkward areas, for example, how much do you want to see her when she is off duty, or how much of the food in the fridge is intended for her?

If you are to be the family's first nanny it may not be a good idea that it is your first job as well. You will not have anyone to guide you and give you confidence in what you are doing as they may be unsure themselves, nor will you have previous job experience to fall back on. You will, however, be free to work out your routine without being compared to previous nannies.

Most first-nanny jobs will be caring for a first child. The parents may naturally be more concerned and protective over their first child than subsequent ones and this over-protectiveness can be difficult to deal with. As their nanny they will look to you for advice and reassurance, and you will have to use all your tact and experience to discuss any problems without hurting their feelings.

As a first nanny with the benefit of previous job experience you may well be more experienced than your new employer in handling likely problems, for example, babysitting, time off, expenses, and so on. You might help by telling her what has worked in the past in previous jobs and then leaving it to her to make up her mind. Some employers allow their nannies a lot of scope for decision-making − if you are a first nanny be prepared for this − you may find yourself deciding everything from feeding patterns to fingernail clipping.

See also: Babies, Household Maintenance, Social Life

Food

Families vary a great deal over what they eat: some live on health foods while others eat anything; some ban sweets while others allow them. You will have to decide, before you accept a job that you like, whether you can live with your prospective family's tastes, because having agreed

to work there you will have to respect their wishes and eat their food.

During the interview you will need to discuss the types of food the children like and how they like it cooked; you could ask for a list before you start the job. Show your employer that you understand varied balanced diets by discussing your food ideas with her. This is also the time to find out if the children have a special diet for health or religious reasons, and to mention yours if you have one, for example, if you are a vegetarian.

In some jobs you will be asked to buy all the food for you and the children; in others it will be bought as part of the family shopping and your expenses will cover any extra food you have to get. If the parents do the food shopping you will need to let them know your requirements so that you can avoid not having enough or the wrong type of food for that particular week. You may of course shop for the whole family — in which case you will need to be aware of their likes and dislikes.

Most jobs work on the arrangement that the nanny either eats with the children, with the parents, or a combination of both. Your accommodation may include cooking facilities. If it does you will be able to cook for yourself and possibly for your friends, but be sure to ask if this is allowed before arranging a dinner party.

DIETING: Trying to diet while working as a nanny is very difficult. If you do put yourself on a diet that requires special food, you should be prepared to pay for it. Do not let the diet affect your job.

Food is an important interview topic; you will hopefully have assessed your nanny's interest and capability then. You will probably rarely be at home when your nanny is cooking for your children and will therefore have to rely on them and her to tell you what they have eaten; if you are particular about this, specify what you want them to eat and when, and leave the food in the fridge; on the other hand, if you trust your nanny and if her knowledge and ideas of what they should eat is in line with yours, you can be more relaxed in your approach. Either way, do not assume that she will give them what you want her to unless she knows what this is and that the issue is important to you.

When she swears blind that she gave them cheese soufflé and the dishwasher is awash with baked bean juice it is time to talk to her.

SWEETS: whatever your policy on sweets may be, be sure your nanny understands and adheres to it; be consistent — if sweets are not allowed when she is looking after them, and you buy them for your children when you are in charge, it will be difficult for her to carry out your wishes. On the other hand, if she ignores your policy, you need to restate it and if necessary explain exactly why you feel the way you do and that you expect her to follow your wishes.

SPECIAL DIETS: If you have a child on a special diet (for example, no E numbers, no milk, and so on) make sure your nanny understands why and that she is prepared to follow it; special diets are usually hard work, particularly if the child is visiting other people's houses — make it easy for your nanny by providing the particular food if possible.

> *Carol had been struggling with her two charges who were having a jelly fight. As her employer came home she was hit by some red flying jelly. There was an embarrassed silence. Carol was dumbstruck but her six-year-old charge piped up: 'Don't worry Mum, there's no E numbers in it.'*

YOUR NANNY'S FOOD: Don't overlook this! If she is vegetarian, don't leave her sausages; ask her what she likes to eat — it may well be very different from your own tastes.

COOKING FOR YOU: This is not a nanny's job, although some enjoy it. If you do want her to cook for you, tell her at the interview — do not spring it on her one night and then take it for granted thereafter.

Marguerite Patten, *Everyday Cook Book* (Hamlyn).
Basic recipes and cooking tips.

First Cookbook (Usborne).
Seven years upwards. Fun and easy recipes, including
basic skills.

You and Your Food (Usborne).
For six years upwards. Explains food including
nutrition, calories, vitamins.

Elisabeth Morse, *My Child Won't Eat* (Penguin).
Common eating problems and practical advice for
dealing with them.

Grandparents

Nannies and grandparents can be great friends or bitter enemies; it can be a difficult balancing act, keeping the peace and listening to both sides of the story, particularly if you are worried about the relationship between you and your nanny and your children. You will need to distinguish between a genuine problem, as raised by a concerned grandparent, and simply a difference of opinion on the way things should be done.

Ask yourself:
- Are your parents or your husband's parents difficult? If so, your nanny will find it as hard to cope with them as you do, particularly if they have firm ideas about child care, rooted in the ideas of fifty years ago. If this is the case, discuss with her how she should deal with any problems they may cause.
- Do they visit a lot or live nearby? If so it may be best if nanny is kept separate from them unless she gets on well with them. Two authority figures together can be confusing for the children and uncomfortable for the nanny.
- Who is in charge when they are around? If it is your nanny then make sure the grandparents understand this and do not undermine her. If you want the grandparents to have the final say, even though your nanny is still on duty, then you must make this clear to your nanny.
- Are your parents criticising your nanny in front of her or behind her back? Make it clear you support her if you can. Try and avoid being pig in the middle.

If you discover at your interview that one or more grandparents lives or is very involved with the family, you will have to establish very clearly how this will affect your working there. It is essential to meet them before deciding to take the job.

It is more likely that you will only have to deal with grandparents over the phone or during the occasional visit. If they are coming to stay you will have to go along with whatever that involves; if the going gets tough, bite your lip and tell yourself it is only a temporary arrangement.

You may be asked to take the children to stay with them; be sure that you are happy about the arrangements before agreeing to go.

When the grandparents live close by do not forget that visiting them can be an enjoyable activity for you all. A grandparent can become a good friend to you and someone to turn to for advice.

Make sure you do not gossip with grandparents about your employers, or the children, as this is unprofessional and may cause family arguments.

Unfortunately some grandparents interfere with what you are doing and give you instructions which they want you to follow. Try to be tactful at the time and work around this, and as soon as you can inform your employer. Ask her how she wants you to respond. Knowing that your employer is aware of the situation and supports you makes things easier to put up with.

It may feel as if the grandparents do not like you, but some do not approve of the mother working, and it is usually the fact that you are there and she is not that they are opposing, rather than you personally.

I know of a granny that rings up the nanny to check the children have their vests on if the month has the letter R in it.

See also: Guests

John Burningham, *Grandpa* (Jonathan Cape).
The boy and his grandpa have magical experiences
before Grandpa dies.

Mari Hedderwick, *Katie Morag and the Two
Grandmothers* (Bodley Head).
Trouble between two grandmothers is solved at the
annual show.

Group Activities

 You will be told at the interview or during the first days
if the children attend any group activities. If so, find
out:

– Where and what time they are held.
– What the children have to take.
– How they are paid for.
– Whether a car run with others is in operation.

If the children do not go to any group activities and the
parents would like them to, you can find out about them
through the children's playgroup or school, from the family's
health visitor, or from local advertisements.

Before committing the child to joining a group you will
probably be able to attend one session with the child, during
which you can satisfy yourself that the group is well run, safe
and worthwhile. Once the child has joined the group the parents
will appreciate hearing how he or she is getting on.

POSSIBLE GROUP ACTIVITIES:
– mother and toddler.– music, choirs.
– sports: e.g. swimming, gymnastics.
– dancing: ballet, tap.
– beavers, cubs, scouts, brownies, and guides.
– first-aid courses: e.g. St John's Ambulance (Badgers),

Junior Red Cross.
– specialised hobbies, e.g. art and craft, stamp collecting.
– environmental organisations: e.g. World Wildlife Fund, RSPB, RSPCA.
– church groups.
– drama groups.

 Whilst group activities are excellent if your child enjoys and learns from them, it is important not to overdo them and unwittingly create a frantic life for him or her. A balance is essential, particularly when the child has school or playgroup to cope with as well.

Your nanny will be in a good position to find out about local activities and monitor them; make sure that she checks the group out for safety, organisation and atmosphere — if she is experienced she will have something to compare the groups with, and know what to look for. Your nanny should not use the group as a chance to put her feet up. Make sure your child is comfortable at the group, and do not hesitate to remove him or her if he or she is not getting anything out of it.

See also: Activities, Cars, Outings

🛈 Helen Pain, *Where to Join* (Northcote House).
A guide to group activities for 9–16-year-olds. Includes addresses.

Guests

Guests' reactions to your nanny can be surprising, helpful, distressing, patronising or a mixture of all of these. Some feel slightly embarrassed that there is an employee in the house and overcompensate by being too friendly; others ignore her or treat her like a servant. Whatever the situation, you can help enormously by making it clear to your guests early on how you feel about her, where she fits into your household and how you expect her to be treated.

It will also help if you make it clear to your nanny, before your guests arrive, who they are, what your relationship is with them, how long they are staying and whether or not she is expected to join you for meals, outings, and so on.

We once had some visitors from Thailand who had servants in their own home. They treated our nanny like a servant, not looking at her when they spoke to her and ordering her around in our absence. Our nanny was new and did not know what to expect in our house. We did not understand why she was being 'off'; when she finally told us what was going on we were horrified and spoke to our guests, but it took a while for the incident to be forgotten. It was deeply offensive to our nanny and very embarrassing for us.

If a guest makes unwelcome advances to your nanny it can be very embarrassing for all and demeaning for the nanny. If you have male friends who do not respect your nanny speak to them about it if you can do so without causing offence; if not, try and arrange for your nanny to be away from the house when that friend is visiting. If you have a good relationship with her you could share the problem with her, making it clear that you support her, and decide on a course of action jointly.

No one else should comment on your nanny's performance to her face unless it is complimentary; if they do, make it clear that you and your nanny solve all problems between you — and then do just that!

Your guest may throw some light on an aspect of your nanny which you did not know about and do not like; if so, providing it is not too serious, tackle the problem after the guest has left and, if possible, do not cite the guest as your source of information.

Your nanny will probably have a lot of guests; it is a good idea to know who these are and have some idea of when they are coming to your house — so that when you walk in on the nanny mafia you are prepared for it and do not feel that you and your house are being taken for granted. There is inevitably something intimidating about a gaggle of gossiping nannies — avoid it if you can!

'Is this what they mean by the "Nanny Mafia"?'

If you are going away and leaving your nanny in charge, you might suggest that she invites friends or family to stay — provided you approve of the visitors she will feel happier and so will you.

Hopefully you will be told beforehand if your employer has guests coming to stay or to visit. Your employer may well ask you to act as hostess on her behalf if her guests are due to arrive while she is not there. You will have little choice over this but should clarify some points first:

– Who is coming and what is your employers' relationship to them?

- Are there any children?
- How much are you expected to do for them, for example, cooking or driving.
- What will they be doing? Will they want to take you/the children out? Are they here for a rest?
- Who has the final say over the children? Should you take instructions from them?
- If they want to take over from you when you are on duty, for example, let you go home early, is it all right to do so?

If your employers' guests are causing you a problem, grit your teeth and bear it if it is only a short visit. Should things become unbearable you will need to find a way of discussing it tactfully.

Remember that the friends you have around on a daily basis for coffee, lunches and teas are guests to the household too. Check that your employer is happy for them to come. While they are with you it is your responsibility to make sure they adhere to the house rules and respect your employers if they meet them.

→ Quick Tip: Don't turn your employers' house into the local café.

As a nanny you may have intimate knowledge of your employers' household; be wary of discussing the family's personal matters with guests. You are in a unique situation which requires a professional attitude.

See also: Grandparents, Privacy

Guilt

You have decided to be a working mother, out of necessity or choice, and you employ a nanny to do many of the things that 'a mother should' for you; nurture your child through the first day at school; make the fancy dress costume; and cheer him or her on at sports day. There are very few of us who can honestly say that we do not, at one time or another, to a greater or lesser degree, feel guilty about our decision to work and handing the responsibility for our child's care and development over to another.

If you feel guilty you may:
- Spoil: giving in to constant demands, allowing the children to stay up late, leave their dinner, and so on, when your nanny has worked to establish discipline in these areas.
- Fuss: constantly ring up or pop in to check up on things, not fully delegating and trusting your nanny.
- Feel insecure: never feel that you do anything properly including, sometimes, relating to and understanding your children.
- Feel threatened: fear that the children will love the nanny more than you.
- Blame yourself when something goes wrong with the children and assume that if you were looking after them all would be well.

One or all of these things can make life difficult for your nanny.

Whilst some nannies are baffled by the mother's guilt and others have a smile about it, a good nanny will have some inkling of what you are feeling and can help you by giving you as much information as possible about the children. Establish early on what you want to know about and create opportunities for her to tell you. It is better for your nanny to volunteer information than for you to be constantly trying to find out what is going on when you are not there. If you feel right about the way your nanny looks after your children, you will feel able to go about your own work reasonably free of guilt.

A good nanny looks after the children – a brilliant nanny looks after the children and your guilt.

Most working parents, particularly the mother, suffer from the guilt of not always being there to look after their children. As a nanny you may be caught in the middle of the mother's need to go to work and her wish to look after her child properly. You are employed to take the mother's place but she may then find it difficult to let you do so. Since most nannies do not have children of their own this guilt can be hard to understand.

As a professional you can help your employer with her guilt feelings by respecting them, and by good communication – volunteering as much information as you can about the children and what they have been doing. Do not wait for your employer to ask – take the chance to show her that you are thinking about the children's welfare, particularly when they are having problems. In this way you will gain your employer's trust, and make it easier for her to delegate the care of the children to you.

See also: Behaviour

 Dr Sirgay Sanger and John Kelly *The Woman Who Works, The Parent Who Cares* (Corgi).
Includes a chapter on feeling guilty about working.

Hairdressers

Taking the children to the hairdressers can be as bad as taking them to the doctor but a bit of forward thinking will help:

- Ask your employer to tell you which hairdressers to use; if anything goes wrong it was their choice!
- It is worth checking more than once exactly what style your employer wants.
- Arrange the appointment for a time when the child is at his or her best, for example after a sleep rather than before.
- When making the appointment, tell the salon it is for a child, as they may have a person who is especially good at handling children.
- Ask how much it will cost and check with your employer that she is happy about it before you go.
- Talk to the child beforehand — say where you are going and why, and offer him or her a treat for afterwards if he or she is good.
- Arriving early is a good idea — it gives the child time to get used to it.
- If you have a particularly difficult child you might find a hairdresser to come to your house.

Every six weeks or so my employer would rush in sporting new highlights, loudly blaming the traffic for being late.

 Quick Tip: Watch children with scissors; after visiting the hairdressers, they all think they are budding stylists!

Make sure you give your nanny clear instructions for your child's haircut — your child may have other ideas and put your nanny in a very embarrassing situation at the hairdressers by insisting that he wants his head shaved when you have asked for a trim.

Cherrystones series, *The Hairdresser* (Hamish Hamilton).
A visit to the hairdressers in photographs.

Holidays

It is generally agreed that a nanny is entitled to the following paid holidays:

- An agreed number of working days — usually a minimum of fifteen — a year.

- Bank holidays: Christmas Day, Boxing Day, New Year's Day, Good Friday, Easter Monday, May Day, Spring Bank Holiday and August Bank Holiday, or a day off in lieu.

These should be discussed fully at the interview, as well as:

- Any previously booked holidays.
- How the holidays are allocated — in the year from the date the nanny starts work or from January to January with any extra months pro rata.
- How the weeks will be taken, for example, two weeks when the employer wants and one when the nanny wants. Some employers will be restricted by their jobs as to when they can take holidays and the nanny will need to work round them; if so, this needs to be clarified at the interview.
- Whether the nanny will go on holiday with her employers' family.

These points should be included in the contract or a side letter.

 THE NANNY'S WORKING HOLIDAY: Holidays taken with the family do not count as part of your annual holiday. Your employers should pay for these holidays but not for your personal expenses.

Going on holiday with the family gives you a marvellous chance to travel and see the world. It is also a break from the normal routine, providing you with an opportunity to gain experience and to get to know the family in relaxed circumstances while having an enjoyable time. You may find yourself sharing a room with the family or rubbing suncream into Dad's back; this familiarity may suit a holiday situation but is not appropriate once you are back at work again.

Don't expect too much:

- It is not your *'real'* holiday — you are there to work.
- If you go on holiday with the family be aware that it will not be easy for you all of the time; you may be with them twenty-four hours a day without a break.
- Going out on your own may not be possible.

– The children may be difficult as they will have all their carers around them at the same time and be in strange surroundings.

Do not take a job on the strength of the holidays being offered to you; the job must have other qualities too since, however attractive they may be, holidays only last for a very short time and are not all as glamorous as they sound.

HOLIDAYS WITH OTHER FAMILIES AND THEIR NANNIES: Some families go on holiday with another family and their nanny; this has advantages if you are already friends. If you do not know the nanny, try to meet her before you go.

Should you go on holiday with another family which does not have a nanny, clarify with your employer before you go what this will mean to you in terms of who you are looking after and when, who is your boss, and whether there will be any extra payment.

Quick Tip: When packing for the children, write out a list and show your employer to make sure you pack everything that she wants.

 Whilst holidays in exotic places are obviously a perk, your holiday is not a holiday for your nanny – she is still on duty, and, however much she may like you, she is not on holiday with friends in a situation of her own choosing. Discuss this beforehand; offer her the chance to come but make it clear that, since she is getting a sort of holiday, she will have to muck in and take her free time to suit your. If you want her to come with you regardless, it is best discussed at the interview if possible. If you can afford it, there are obvious advantages to taking your nanny with you on holiday; apart from having an extra pair of hands on the journey, you will be free to have a lie-in or go out without the children, or with individual children, when you want to.

However, remember that your nanny will need time off during the holiday but may have no one to enjoy it with – this can lead to you feeling guilty and bending over backwards to make sure she has a good time. You will also have less chance to be alone with the children in relaxed circumstances.

See also: Contract, Interviews

Susan Grossman, *Have Kids Will Travel* (Macdonald).

David Haslam, *Travelling With Children* (Macdonald).

David McPhail, *First Flight* (Blackie).
A boy and his teddy go for their first flight on an aeroplane.

Hours

If you are aiming to keep your nanny for as long as possible, be meticulous about the way you deal with her hours and adhere to what was agreed in her contract – not doing so is one of the biggest employer 'sins' and contributes to more nannies leaving jobs than employers realise.

Don't:
- Officially agree shorter hours than are realistic. If you know you are likely to be able to get home at 6 pm, employ her until 6.30 pm; she will be pleased to be let off early but dismayed by you constantly coming in at 6.15.
- Forget that she has a private life and is entitled to be able to make arrangements and be reasonably sure of sticking to them.
- Take the extra time she puts in for granted – give her time off in lieu or pay her overtime if you can afford to.
- Come home later than agreed without ringing to say so.
- Assume she is on duty just because she is not going out that night.
- Forget to apologise if you are late home.

Quick Tip: Be strict with her and strict with yourself. Be generous where you can.

 For most nannies long hours are the biggest drawback to their chosen career; they are something you have to accept as being unique to a nanny's job.

Discussing your hours fully at the interview and having them written into the contract will give you something to refer to if any problems arise. Clarify what 'approximately' really means. Whilst it is not appropriate or realistic to timecheck yourself on and off duty, you do need to know where you stand with regard to working late and to feel that your employer respects your social life.

If your employer is often late home and obviously not making an effort to keep to your hours, you will have to rediscuss the situation.

 Quick Tip: Always be punctual.

See also: Communication, Contracts, Interviews

Household Maintenance

 When starting a new job it is a good idea to find out what household appliances you will be expected to use, how they work, and where spare parts like batteries or bulbs are kept.

Changing hoover bags, or emptying dishwasher and tumble-dryer filters may not seem like part of your job but if you use the appliances, and you will probably do so more than your employer, it is worthwhile doing this as an insurance against the greater inconvenience if the machine breaks down.

If you think a machine is not functioning properly mention this to your employer straight away rather than hoping that it will go wrong when they are using it.

Should the machine go seriously wrong when your employers are not around, do not attempt to mend it yourself unless you are sure of what to do. Where possible contact your employers for their authorisation before you call out a repair man.

You may have a conversation something like this:

Nanny:	The washing machine has broken and it's leaking all over the kitchen floor.
Employer:	Oh no! What did you do to it?
Nanny:	Nothing.
Employer:	Well — it's been working perfectly well for me while you've been away.
Nanny:	Well it's not now! And I've used it as I usually do.
Employer:	OK then, you'd better call the plumber.

→ **Quick Tip:** Do not attempt any repairs yourself — unless you have an 'A' level in plumbing or metalwork.

 If you are to keep your children and your nanny safe it is essential that all appliances are well maintained and that your nanny knows how to use them properly. She may not have any experience of some of the machinery you take for granted, for example, dishwashers, coffee percolators, juice extractors and so on. Take time to make sure she understands how to work them. Leave the instruction leaflets where she has access to them.

Whilst you may be cursed with a particularly clumsy nanny, try to avoid the only natural tendency to think that when something breaks down it was her fault — your nanny probably uses your household machinery more than you do and therefore statistically there is more chance of a breakdown occurring when she is using it than when you are.

See also: **Breakages, Callers, Communication, First Job, Insurance**

Illness

If you are ill you are entitled to time off work, but if you are a live-in nanny this means having that time off ill at your work place; your employer may have to take time off to cover for you, which may not be possible. Therefore employers often ask you to try and carry on when you are ill. If this is the case then you could ask your nanny friends to help out. If you are too ill to work you will do best to go home if you can – your employers will have to find another way of coping.

'*Poor* Nanny! Fancy having chicken-pox! Take it easy today. Don't worry about the dishes'.

If you develop a serious or infectious condition you have an obligation to inform your employer.

ILLNESS IN THE FAMILY: If a child has a serious illness or has to go into hospital, you can help by giving the family lots of reassurance and support. Keep your daily routine as normal as possible, and help arrange visits to the hospital. If there are other children in the family, be aware of their needs, they will require extra care and attention at this difficult time too. If either of your employers is ill, keep the children away from them and hope that they soon recover.

When your nanny comes down with 'flu just as you are leaving for a vital meeting with your boss you have a problem; most nannies end up struggling through coughs and colds since there is often no viable alternative, particularly at the last moment. It is short-sighted and unfair to ask your nanny to work on if she is really poorly — she will take longer to recover and not be able to do her work as efficiently. It is a good idea to prepare for these moments by having a contingency for emergencies up your sleeve; relatives and friends might help out, or (this is where the nanny network comes into its own) other nannies may be able to help. As a last resort, you could employ a temp through an agency. It obviously becomes difficult if the period of illness is lengthy since few employers can afford to pay both nanny and temporary replacement for very long.

SICK PAY: The issue of sick pay is often overlooked by both employers and nannies. The payment of sick pay is dependent on the contract of employment and should be clarified at the interview. Most employers continue to pay their nanny her full wage if she is off sick for less than a week.

The mechanics of sick pay can be confusing. You will need to know:

1. *Is your nanny eligible for sick pay?* A nanny is eligible for Statutory Sick Pay (SSP) after working for an employer for one day if she officially earns more than the National Insurance Contributions (NIC) lower earnings limit, and provided she is not over sixty,

self-employed or contracted for less than thirteen weeks.

2. *Who pays when the nanny is sick?* The employer pays SSP and can then claim 80 per cent of the total gross SSP back. Deduct this from your NI contributions and tax which you send to the Inland Revenue. The employer makes the returns on the nanny's deduction card and should keep SSP records in front of the payslip booklet.

3. *How much is SSP?* In 1991 it is £52.50 for nannies earning £185 plus, £43.50 for nannies earning between £52 and £184.99. This is updated on 6 April each year; you can get further information from your local social security office who will give you the leaflet 'Statutory Sick Pay Rates and Notes' to help you.

4. *Does the employer have to pay anything?* This is dependent upon what has been agreed and included in the contract. However, it would be a mean employer who did not contribute something and ideally she should top the SSP up to the nanny's full wage for the first four weeks if the nanny has been in the job for thirteen weeks, and for the first eight weeks if the nanny has been in the job over a year.

    Make sure you have both thought through the implications of this before agreeing to include it in the contract; an employer may not be able to afford two nannies' salaries for this length of time and will need to balance the need to be fair with her ability to pay.

5. *When is SSP payable?* After four consecutive days' illness, (including the weekend) and once you have been ill for three qualifying days (days on which you would have worked had you not been ill). In those first four days a good employer will pay the full wage and this is normal practice, but legally they are not obliged to pay anything.

    For example, a nanny who works Monday to Friday and becomes ill on Thursday and returns to work on the following Wednesday will have her SSP calculated as follows:

Thursday - Sunday inclusive are her four consecutive days' illness.
Thursday, Friday, Monday are her qualifying days.
SSP is paid for *Tuesday* only.

'There doesn't seem to be anything here about the headache all this gives to the bosses'.

6. *How long is SSP payable for?* Up to twenty-three weeks.
7. *Does the employer have to keep records?* Yes. An SSP record sheet is available at the DSS and records have to be kept for at least three years after the end of the tax year; the employer is risking a fine if these records are not kept.
8. *Is SSP subject to deductions?* Yes — both tax and National Insurance contributions are deducted by the employer who will be able to claim the employer's NI contributions back when making quarterly returns.
9. *When is a doctor's note necessary?* After seven days' illness.
10. *What further information is available?* Full details of how SSP is paid can be obtained from your local DSS; the Social Security Advice Line for Employers (0800 393539) also offers advice.

See also: Contracts, Doctors, Interviews

Franz Brandenberg, *I Don't Feel Well* (Puffin).
Edward isn't well and Elizabeth is jealous.

Helen Nicoll and Jan Pienkowski, *Mog's Mumps*
(Puffin).

Jill Black, *The Working Mother's Survival Guide* (Simon
and Schuster).
Includes a section on SSP.

DSS Leaflet Section,
PO Box 21,
Stanmore,
Middlesex HA7 1AY

Insurance

Insurance can be an area which gets overlooked until it is too
late. It is worth considering the different types of insurance
policies which relate to a nanny/employer situation.

NANNY'S INJURY

Public Liability Insurance: This insures the employer against
claims for injury, death or disease by the nanny.

When an employer employs a nanny she must inform her
household insurance company who will confirm whether or not
the nanny is covered under her policy, and will issue her with an
Employers and Public Liability Insurance Certificate which
should, officially, be displayed in the house.

The premium, if any, will depend on the individual insurance
company and her existing insurance cover with them. If she
does not inform them she runs the risk of any claim resulting
from employing her nanny being invalidated.

CHILDREN'S INJURY IN NANNY'S CARE

Professional Negligence Insurance: This insures the nanny against any claims which may be made as a result of the children being injured or killed whilst in her care. Contact your local insurance broker or Robert Barrow (see below), a broker who offers advice on all types of insurance cover for nannies, including professional malpractice.

If the nanny is a member of a union she is automatically covered should an employer bring an action against her alleging professional negligence.

In practice few nannies and employers bring cases against each other since proving negligence is a difficult and costly process.

NANNY'S AND EMPLOYER'S PROPERTY

Household Insurance: This is insurance which insures the employer against damage to or theft of her property. The employer should check that her insurance does indeed cover her nanny for accidental damage and theft.

CAR INSURANCE

If the nanny is to drive the children around in her own or her employer's car, she must be insured. The employer can extend her own insurance to include the nanny, and the nanny can extend hers to cover business use if necessary. It is useful where relevant for both parties to have seen the insurance documents and know that you and the children are properly covered.

See also: Accidents, Bereavement, Breakages, Cars

Robert Barrow Limited,
24-26 Minories,
London EC3N 1BY
Tel: 071 709 9611.

Interviews

 Young women take up nannying for a variety of different reasons. Some do so because they love and want to work with children; some because they trained as nursery nurses and there are not enough nursery jobs to go round; some because they want to travel; some because they want experience of working with children prior to setting up their own nurseries or going into teacher training, and some for want of a better thing to do.

As employers of nannies, we must be realistic in what we expect; we cannot take it for granted that a nanny will be with us for a very long period of time since most like to move on to a new challenge once they have reached their natural peak in a job (which can be anything from three months to three years or more, depending on you, your treatment of them, your children, your nanny's personality and personal circumstances.)

When you are interviewing for your first nanny and may not have had any experience of interviewing before, you will need to bear the above in mind. Do not be surprised if your ideal nanny does not materialise at the interview — be prepared to compromise where you can and be wary of projecting the qualities you are looking for on to your interviewee.

The type of nanny you employ will obviously depend on your specific circumstances: the number and ages of your children, the demands of your job, the size of your house and your income, and your feelings and ideas about the care of your children. Much of this will have been reflected in your advertisement, but do not be surprised if nannies telephone you who do not exactly meet the requirements you asked for; you will need to decide how important those requirements are and whether it is worth interviewing someone who is not really what you had in mind. If you feel that she is not for you on the telephone you can be almost certain that you will be wasting time for both of you giving her an interview.

THE TELEPHONE CALL: This is an important part of the interviewing process. It is useful to weed out the no-hopers on the telephone, thus saving everyone time and embarrassment. Have a list of questions you want to ask them when they telephone and use a separate sheet for each call; you can then use this when the nanny comes to be interviewed.

Briefly find out:

- Name, age, address.
- Qualifications, experience, including the number of jobs and how long they spent in each.
- The ages, numbers and sexes of the children they have cared for, and whether or not they have experience of your children's age and age gap.
- How long they are intending to stay.
- If they hold a driving licence, and how long they have been driving.
- If they have any references.

Be wary of those who only have 'babysitting' experience and make sure you understand what the various qualifications are — some courses concentrate on care in general and not children in particular. Establish which course the nanny did, where, exactly what it involved and what particular aspects she enjoyed about it. This will help you confirm that her qualification is relevant. Some nannies have been known, when asked whether they are qualified, to say yes but omit to say what in; if the employer does not ask any further questions she may never find out that the qualification was, in fact, a hairdressing one.

Since good nannies are not always easy to come by, bear in mind that you are selling yourself to your prospective employees as much as they are doing the same to you. Have a list of the main points of the job you are advertising by the phone so that you can give as much information as possible: the children, your job, hours, time off, car, holidays, accommodation, and so on.

If you are asking someone to come for an interview from a long way away you should consider paying her fares. Do not be surprised if some of your interviewees do not turn up. Nannies are not always good at cancelling appointments; it is an infuriating habit, particularly if you have rushed round frantically making house and children presentable.

THE FIRST INTERVIEW: It is a good idea to use the information you got on the phone and add to it at the interview. Apart from the intuitive things such as whether you like her, whether you can trust her with your home and children, whether the children like her, and whether you can cope with her round the house on a daily basis, you should find out the potential nanny's knowledge of and/or attitude to:

- Safety, for example, when out shopping, bathtime, medicines, in the car.
- First aid.
- Discipline, for example, using 'yes' more than 'no', smacking.
- Potty training.
- Child development/Creative activities — is she interested and does she enjoy it? Her answer to this question may give you an idea of the extent of her knowledge, ability,

motivation, enthusiasm for and understanding of children.

- Television — will she use it as a babysitter? and what programmes does she think are appropriate for your children?
- Food — does she understand nutritional needs, and does she enjoy cooking?
- Activities — is she happy to take the children swimming, to the park etc.?
- Books — does she enjoy reading to children? What are her favourite children's books?

It is also useful to find out: (either by asking or observation):

- Why is she a nanny — what does she enjoy about the job?
- What qualities does she consider important in a nanny?
- Is she prepared to do the rotten jobs as well as the enjoyable ones with a good grace?
- Will she have a routine? Ask her to talk you through it if you are in any doubt.
- Is she organised and efficient? Creative? Resourceful?
- Has she dealt with your age child before? Does this matter?
- If a driver, how long has she held her driving licence? Has she had any accidents?
- Does she smoke? If so, is she prepared not to while on duty?
- Does she have the specific skills you are looking for, for example, experience of newborn babies.
- Will she get bored and moan a lot or is she cheerful, reliable and a pleasure to have in the house? Beware the disgruntled nanny — she can sour the atmosphere for the whole family just by her presence.
- Does she really want the job?
- Is her health good? Has she had any major operations?
- What is her social life like? Does she have a boyfriend or several and how often does she see him/them?
- How does she speak of her previous employers? Be wary

of the nanny who badmouths them — it may be your turn
next.
- Will she fit in? Is her background totally different to yours
and does this matter? There may well be differences in
your nanny's attitude to food, religion, politics,
behaviour, use of language, sex, swearing.

'And I like to knit and read in the evenings'.

- What does she do in her spare time? Will she be out of the
house at the weekends and in the evenings or staying at
home watching TV? What sort of nanny are you looking
for?

- Will she do what you want her to even though she may
not necessarily share your views?
- Is she stable, or are you just taking on another child?
- Will she be independent; does this matter?
- What will she do at weekends?
- Is she going to be flexible?
- Could she cope in an emergency?

→ Quick Tip: Ask to see her qualifications, driving licence, references and c.v. if she has one. Give her something else to do while you read them, for example, playing with the children.

Although you may find it embarrassing, it is also advisable to ask:

- Has she any dependants, for example, her own children?
- Has she any children in care?
- Has she ever had any criminal convictions?

WHAT TO TELL HER

- Terms and conditions, including full details of length of employment, notice period, wages, tax, National Insurance, hours, holidays, sick pay, pensions and sackable offences — and whether or not these are stated in a contract and/or letter.
- Duties in full, warts and all. If you gloss over the unpleasant bits, or even fail to mention them, they will be resented once they are discovered and this will sow the seeds of distrust between you and your nanny.
- Do not make false promises (for example, that you'll buy her a new car after the trial period). If you do not stick to your word, why should she? Both nannies and employers intensely dislike the feeling of being conned; the more you say one thing and do another, the greater that feeling.
- Inform her about the local nanny network if you know of one.

If you like her it is often best to offer the job then and there; she may be going on to another job interview which will offer better pay and conditions and you may lose her.

If you instinctively do not like a nanny in the first five minutes cut the interview short. Stop asking questions yourself and ask her if she has any questions for you. You can then answer them briefly and terminate the interview.

Be absolutely clear about everything and do not leave anything open to misinterpretation; it is better to paint a 'worst case' picture, and have her pleasantly surprised later, than a rosy one which is not true and leads to distrust and disillusion once the reality becomes clear.

Whilst you may like to have the children around during the interview, depending on their ages, you may prefer to avoid unsettling them until you have selected the possible candidates for the job; this applies particularly if the children are old enough to understand what is happening and are resistant to the situation. The only disadvantage if you do this is that the potential nanny cannot judge the most important part of her job. One way to overcome this problem is to have the children looked after for the first part of the interview and then let them meet the nanny if she is a possible employee.

You will learn a lot about the nanny from your children's reaction to her and the way she approaches them; be aware, however, that she knows she is being watched and so her behaviour may be stilted — although a 'natural' nanny will make headway whatever the situation. If you have children who are mature enough, it can be a good idea to involve them in the choice of their nanny.

THE SECOND INTERVIEW: Many employers interview a prospective nanny for the second time, sometimes having her stay for a day or for tea in a more relaxed environment than the first interview. This second interview is excellent if you are not absolutely sure about her, and gives you a chance to tell her about the job in more detail, clarifying any of the grey areas, for example, sick pay, emptying the bins, or feeding the dog. You will need to make it clear how much initiative you want your prospective nanny to show in this situation. It can be awkward for a nanny to take charge, not knowing whether she should do so or not.

Many unhappy job situations could be avoided if nannies took more care over the interview and were honest with their employers and, most importantly, themselves. Many nannies take a job knowing that they are not clear or happy about several points but hoping that these can be sorted out at another date or that they will never arise. The problems will almost certainly get bigger and result in a very unpleasant time for all, ending with you either leaving or being asked to leave what otherwise might have been a very happy job.

Whilst it is a good idea to arrange interviews in the same area on the same day do not arrange too many. It will become difficult to take all the information in, and you will get muddled over which job offered what.

Good preparation for an interview is essential. Allow yourself plenty of time to get ready and think through what you want to ask, say, do and wear.

THE TELEPHONE CALL: The telephone call you make in answer to an advert will be your first contact with the employer. Do not dismiss this as unimportant; the impression you make during this call may get you the job and you can also get an idea of the basic terms and conditions offered. Have your opening sentence ready and sound positive and interested.

Make a list of your priorities, which may include some or all of the following:

- Type of job; sole charge, live in or out.
- Children: names, ages and sex.
- Hours: what are they, how much time off will you have, and will you be needed at weekends?
- Babysitting: how often will you be needed and will you be paid for it?
- Duties: nursery duties only or others as well?
- Start date.
- Parents' names, jobs, where they work.
- Where do they live and what is it like?
- Wages.
- Car: is one available?
- Accommodation: what does this consist of?
- Trial period: is there one and if so, how long is it?
- Minimum length of time required to stay.

– Holidays: how many weeks paid holiday will you have?

 Quick Tip: Do not be afraid to say at this stage if it does not sound like the job for you.

If you are offered a further interview, make sure you write down:
- Name.
- Address of house.
- Directions.
- Time of interview.

The cost of getting to the interview may sometimes be met by the interviewer. This depends on the distance you are travelling and whether you are seeing other prospective employers. Where the interviews are local most nannies bear the costs themselves.

WHAT TO WEAR: Most employers are looking for a positive, cheerful, reliable, fun, caring person to look after their children. The way you look reflects the sort of person you are and the first impression can make the difference between getting or not getting the job.

Your clothes should be comfortable and give you confidence but also be practical in case you have a chance to play with the children. If you want to wear trousers it is probably better that they are not jeans. Employers notice nannies' shoes, so make sure these are suitable too. If you have a uniform you may like to wear that.

THE JOURNEY: Before leaving check that you have:
- References.
- Your c.v.
- Qualification certificates.
- Directions.
- List of questions and notepad – if you think you will forget to ask questions or remember what you have been told.

When working out the journey time be generous to allow for hold-ups. On the way make a mental note of what you see; it may help you when deciding whether to take the job or not. Note:

- The area: is it country, town, isolated. Do you like it?
- Facilities: cinema, swimming pool, theatre, parks. Will they be accessible to you?
- Length of journey: This is essential if you want to go home at weekends or if it is a live-out job.

THE FIRST INTERVIEW:

 Quick Tip: Smile when they open the door to you.

You will probably be feeling quite nervous, but try to stay calm and be yourself. During the interview you will be asked a lot of questions — be prepared for this. Answer these questions honestly and not with one-word answers. Do not be afraid to talk about your experiences where relevant and to show initiative, for example, when a child needs help, offer it. If you are left with the children at any time, talk to and play with them; you will be able to find out about them and create a good impression at the same time. Ideally, you will be able to meet both parents and all the children during the interview.

The interview is a two-way process. It is important that you ask as well as answer questions. You may need to be assertive if you are not clear about something, do not feel you understand what is being said, or sense that you are not being told the whole story. It is too late once you have started work. Your first impression of the family and job are very important — do not ignore your instincts. Throughout the interview remind yourself that you will have to work closely and perhaps live with them, so you must like and feel comfortable with them.

During the interview be aware of the general atmosphere in

the house, of how the interview is being conducted, of the language being used, and of the attitude shown towards you. This will help you to build up a general impression of the family and help you decide if you would fit in.

Below is a list of extra points to add to the basic details you found out during the telephone call. You should clarify the basic points again and discuss these. You will find out the answers to some questions just by looking and listening.

THE CHILDREN:

- Do the children attend school, playgroup, or any other clubs?
- Do the children have an active social life, friends, hobbies, and favourite activities? This will give you a good idea of what the job will involve.
- What does the daily routine involve?
- Do the children have allergies, special diets, medication, or special needs?
- Are there any extra children to be cared for on a regular basis or in the holidays? There may be stepchildren, or older children at boarding-school.

Ask yourself: do you like the children? Have you had experience of this age group? Could you cope with them? Are you willing and able to provide for their particular likes and needs, for example, swimming?

THE PARENTS:

- What do they like to be called?
- Do other people work for them in their jobs? It is a bonus if they do as they will be used to handling staff and therefore hopefully better at handling you.
- How involved do they want to be when they are at home?

What is their attitude to:

- Daily routine: how flexible are they?
- Food: are there any specific rules or special diets?
- Discipline: do they have any fixed ideas?
- Activities: educational, social and play.
- Television: is it allowed, how much, and which programmes?
- Going out: will you be allowed to take the children out and where?
- Health: are there any problems and do they cope well if so?
- Boyfriends.
- Girlfriends.

Ask yourself: Do you like them? Could you work for them, and will you respect them? How are they with the children: fussy, worried, calm, fanatical? Do they really need a nanny and understand all that that means, for example, the cost, lack of privacy and need for trust? How do they speak of the last nanny? Be wary of a lot of negative comments.

TERMS AND CONDITIONS: You should clarify the information you were given on the telephone and also find out about the following:

- Car: including usage, petrol and insurance.
- Contract and side letter; is there one and what will be included in it?
- Friends — are there any other local nannies?
- House rules: what are they?
- Leaving: how much notice will be given by either side?
- Other staff employed, for example, a cleaner.
- Pets: will you be required to care for them?
- Tax, National Insurance and sick pay: will these be paid?
- Clothes: what will you be expected to wear?

Ask yourself: Do you understand exactly what you are being asked to do? Are you happy with these conditions? Are you happy to compromise on some of them?

THE HOUSE:

- Ask to see your accommodation.
- Where else in the house can you go?
- What can you use in the house?
- Garden. A good garden that is safe and provides a play area is a bonus.

By the end of an interview you will have a feeling for whether or not you would like the job. What happens next will vary. You may be offered the job on the spot: unless you are very sure, ask to have time to think about it. You may have other interviews to attend. Your interviewer will probably have other nannies to see and will arrange to ring you when she has come to a decision. Check that she has your telephone number and tell her the best time to ring. (If you have not told your current employer you are leaving, this should obviously not be when she is at home.) If you would like the job but are not offered it then and there, try to find the opportunity to say how you feel; if an employer is wavering but knows that you are interested, that may help her make her mind up.

In some cases you may be asked to attend a second interview, or if offered the job you may like to have a second look and clear up any queries you have. If at any time you decide not to take the job it is courteous and professional to let the family know.

See also: Activities, Advertisements, Babysitting, Bathrooms, Bedrooms, Boyfriends, Cars, Contracts, Child Development, Clothes, Curriculum Vitae, Discipline, Duties, Extra Children, Holidays, Hours, Illness, Leaving, Pets, Safety, Social Life, Tax and National Insurance, Television, Training, Type of Job, Wages, Weekends

---

 Clive Fletcher, *How to Face the Interview* (Unwin). Chapters include approach, first step, preparation, the interview and reviewing.

Judy Skeats, *Interviews* (Ward Lock Ltd). 'How to succeed'.

Kitchens

Leaving

There are many reasons for leaving a job; you may want a change – different children and circumstances – more money, more responsibility, wider experience, travel, a move into a different area of child care, or a chance to work abroad.

When you are trying to work out when you will leave, think of the children and where possible choose a good time for them, for example, not near exam times or other changes.

If you are confident that your leaving will be accepted and your notice period honoured, be honest with the family from the start. Tell them as soon as you decide to leave; this is never easy. In the first instance you may feel happier telling just one employer. Do not be surprised if they are not overjoyed, however nice they are or however well you get on with them; a nanny leaving creates a stressful and difficult time for a family. Provided you have given the agreed amount of notice, once they have got used to the idea of your leaving most employers are reasonable. If you can give more notice than you agreed you will help your employer, since it takes anything up to eight weeks to replace a permanent nanny.

Some nannies are treated badly when they hand in their notice; being told to leave immediately, having to cope with a bad atmosphere for the notice period, not being paid, or not being given a reference. If you feel that your employers might react badly to your handing in your notice you may decide to be further on in the leaving process before you tell them. This could include first checking that there are suitable jobs in the area you want to go to, joining an agency, or attending some interviews. If you do this and get offered a job, remember that you must still work your agreed notice period. If your notice period is, for example, four weeks, tell your new employers that you need to give four clear weeks' notice (which may mean more than four weeks in practice).

You may want to leave the job earlier than you agreed because you have had a string of problems that are not resolving themselves, and you are feeling frustrated and taken for granted. Before you give up be sure that you have tried to tackle the situation and resolve it with your employer and it is not just a case of her being unaware that you are not happy. If you have tried and failed to solve your problems, and still want to leave, you are probably better to do so. However, it is important to honour your notice period. Nannies who do not work their notice period or leave unannounced and make their employers angry are letting themselves, other nannies, and the reputation of the profession down.

If you are asked to leave before your notice period ends, your employers should pay you your wage until the agreed date.

TELLING THE CHILDREN: You may find the worst part of leaving is telling the children, handling their questions and coping with your own feelings. It is a good idea to discuss in detail with your employers what line you will all take with the children, before attempting to tell them. Be sure to tell them early enough so they have enough time to get used to the idea. Make it clear that you are not leaving because of something they have done and be prepared to listen to their fears and give lots of reassurance. Do not talk about your new job to your friends in front of the children.

Whilst people may think it odd for you to feel guilty and upset at leaving a job which you perhaps did not enjoy much, it is only natural to feel like this; you are leaving children that you have become very close to and who you know will miss you and you them. If you need to, have a good cry, preferably away from your friends and colleagues who may well not understand, and do not feel badly about it. Whilst you may have learned 'not to get too close to the children' in your training you may well have found this impossible in reality; leaving children you love hurts and it is only human to feel upset: but do not let this affect the children.

Having handed in your notice, try to keep up the same standards that you have had throughout the job; if your work goes downhill your employer is left with that memory instead of remembering your good work.

Leave the job as you would wish to find it. This will give the new nanny an easier start and you a sense of completion. Leave the playrooms and bedrooms tidy and sorted out, and make sure that all the clothes are washed and ironed. Offer to write a brief description of your daily routine and any other helpful hints you can think of, for example, where to park at the school, how to kick the dishwasher three times to get it to start, and not to leave the dog in the kitchen when you go out. Also include a list of the names and telephone numbers of other nannies/mothers, and the children's friends. It is not a good idea to include your personal opinions, or make the information too detailed.

 Quick Tip: Do not forget to leave the children's library tickets.

 'I had no idea she was unhappy'.
'We've treated her well – I can't understand why she wants to move on'.
'She just suddenly announced she was leaving in two weeks' time, even though we had agreed four weeks' notice.'

Employers are very often baffled when their apparently contented nanny announces that she is leaving. It does not matter how hard you prepare yourself for your nanny leaving, the announcement always comes as a shock, followed by feelings of anger, rejection, panic and 'Why me? Why now? Just when . . .'. There is usually a good reason for the nanny's departure, in her terms, which the employer has never thought about (since she rarely views her nanny's job from her nanny's point of view). However, it is also true that nannies often let the side down when it comes to leaving and do not take into consideration what it will mean for their employers.

Nannies do move on, but you can help minimise the upheaval. Stress to her that leaving you will not be a problem but not giving sufficient notice will. Nannies are aware that some employers behave badly when they hand in their notice and this may affect the way they do so, even if you have every intention of being civilised about it. Fears of being thrown out without pay, at worst, may lead them to look after number one at the expense of a proper notice period. It will help you if you do not expect her to stay forever and are one step ahead, keeping an eye out for problems which may make her want to move on.

When she hands her notice in:
  − Discuss the fact that the next few weeks may feel a bit difficult and odd with your nanny. Try to work together.
  − Decide with your nanny how and when the children should be told.

- Discuss her possibly visiting the children, if she wants to, once the new nanny has settled in and they have accepted her.
- Give her a reference, mentioning length of service, capability, relationship with the children, relationship with you, attitude and personality.

If you were happy with your nanny, writing her reference will be easy; if you were not, you can describe her duties rather than how well she performed them. If you would not recommend her as a nanny — don't!

Once she has gone and life has settled down again, you may well look back and realise that the last few months had not been as good as the first and that her leaving was not such a bad thing. Most nanny / employer relationships, however good, have a limited lifespan and it helps to be aware of this from the start.

DISMISSAL:

Define your grounds for dismissal in her contract; you will then have a case if you have to dismiss her.

If your nanny is guilty of gross misconduct she can be sacked without notice or payment. You will need to decide what you consider to be gross misconduct; theft, cruelty and drunkenness are most frequently given as examples.

Other offences which might lead to dismissal vary greatly from family to family, and may include:

- Failure to comply with instructions and procedures, for example, disregarding house rules.
- Unreliability in time-keeping or attendance.
- Disrupting the household, for example, making advances to the father.
- Job incompetence.
- Behaving during or outside working hours in a way which might harm the reputation of the employer.

You will need to decide what you want to include in the contract. Before a nanny can be sacked for these or other offences, her employer has to give her one oral warning, followed by a written warning. If her behaviour does not improve after these warnings she can be sacked.

You may be reluctant to dismiss your nanny, particularly if she gets on well with the children, as it will mean an unsettling change in their lives. However, trust your instincts; do not hesitate to dismiss her over something serious, however much you or your children like the nanny.

If you have to dismiss her:

 – Prepare the ground if you have time, lining up a temp or cover from friends/relatives.
 – Do not do it in front of the children; however bad the situation is, they have been cared for by her and may be very attached to her whatever her shortcomings.
 – Be careful how you give her a reference, if at all.
 – If it is not dismissal for gross misconduct, you must pay her for her notice period, even if you do not require her to work it.

If you feel you have been dismissed unfairly it is best to tell the agency you got the job through, so that they can form their own opinion, help you, and place the next nanny accordingly. If asked, you will need to explain to your new employers what happened too – it is better that they hear it from you, from the start, rather than learn it from another source.

If you are a member of a union, they will help you with unfair dismissal and if not, your local Citizens' Advice Bureau can advise you. You cannot take your employers to an industrial tribunal for unfair dismissal unless you have been working for them for more than two years.

REDUNDANCY

A nanny's time with her employers is limited by:

 – The nature of the job: eventually the children go to school full time and the nanny is not needed.
 – Few nannies stay in their jobs for longer than two years.

If however, a nanny is made redundant and she has worked for the family for more than two years and is aged eighteen or over, redundancy payment is currently calculated as follows:

- Half a week's pay for every year if you are aged eighteen—twenty-one inclusive.
- One week's pay for every year if you are aged twenty-two—forty inclusive.
- One and a half week's pay if you are aged forty-one—sixty-four.

Payment is also due for any notice period not worked in addition to the redundancy payment.

See also: Bereavement, Contracts, New Job/New Nanny, Overlapping, Questions, Unions

Moving House

At your interview you should be told if the family are planning to move in the near future and where and when this will be. If you then take on the job you must be prepared to help with the move and stay with the family once they have moved.

If the family you are working for decides to move, you are not obliged to move with them unless it is written in your contract or you want to. You may want to consider moving with them initially and helping the children adjust to their new home before leaving.

Should you decide to move with the family, it is wise to see the new house and your accommodation for yourself first.

The children may be insecure about moving; you will be able to reassure them by talking it through, perhaps using books to help explain what is happening. Let them help you to pack and unpack their belongings so that they feel that some things, for example, their toys, are staying the same. Be prepared for behaviour changes from the children as a result of the move, and for a period of adjustment while they get used to new friends, schools and activities.

If you move house and your nanny moves with you, you will need to reassess your nanny's terms and conditions. Will her accommodation be similar? Are her hours going to be the same? Will she need to drive if she did not need to before? If she is substantially less well off as a result of the move and you want to keep her, consider a rise. Remember it may take her time to adjust to the new environment.

See also: Group Activities, Schools, Working Abroad

Nigel Snell *Sally Moves House* (Hamish Hamilton).
For younger children.

Kate Petty and Lisa Kopper, *Moving House* (Franklin Watts).
Helps to explain what moving will involve to the young child.

Diana Hendry, *The Not Anywhere Tree* (Julia MacRae).
For older children a story about moving.

New Job/New Nanny

This section applies to second and subsequent jobs / nannies.
Some of the information found under FIRST JOB and FIRST
NANNY will apply to this situation as well.

It will not help you to compare your new job with your
last one, for better or worse. Each family is unique;
allow yourself time to adjust. During your first days in
a new job you may feel nervous and awkward and wonder why
you left your last job, where at least you knew the routine even
if there may have been problems. You may also miss your old
charges, friends and situations. These feelings will be mixed
with the excitement of new prospects and wanting to meet the
new challenge; and the experience from your old job will help
you a great deal in your new situation.

In the early days of your new job:

- Be prepared for the children to test you.
- Do not get upset if the children reject you, call you by the
  other nanny's name or ask you when you are leaving.
- Consider how they are feeling; they may be feeling
  insecure, guilty, abandoned, missing their old nanny and
  routine.
- Do not rush to establish your routine; take your cues from
  the children and expect the change to be gradual.
- Be aware of the balance between pleasing/impressing
  them and establishing a firm and fair routine/relationship
  for the future. For example, do not run round clearing all
  their toys up after them every day for a week if you want
  them to help with these things once you are established in
  the job.
- Try not to show your fears, or even unhappiness. Be
  positive and cheerful.

– Answer their questions and talk about the enjoyable
   things that you will do in the future.

One temporary nanny walked into the house one morning after the
weekend to hear:

Boy: *Who's that, Mummy?*
Mother: *That's your new nanny, Gill.*
Boy: *Oh No!! I thought we'd changed that one.*

A new nanny can be a blessing or a worry; if your
outgoing nanny was brilliant and you are sad to see her
go, you will find it hard to adapt to a new one and may
be tempted to compare her with the old. If, however, you are
glad to see the back of your old nanny, then the new one
represents new hope for the future and you may be tempted to
project the qualities you really wanted in the old one on to her.
Either situation can be difficult – how will the children cope?
How will you get on with her? Will she be as good as she
seemed at the interview? There is one bonus – you are now
experienced in employing a nanny in your own home; you may
well have learned to compromise; you will have learned when to
put your foot down and when to hold back; and you will
probably have a more realistic picture of what employing a
nanny is about.

There is a temptation to imagine that the new nanny will not
only not have the faults of the old one, but will have no faults at
all. Each nanny has her own strengths and weaknesses; you may
avoid making the same mistakes you made with the first one but
make others in your effort to 'get it all right this time'. Do not
judge her by or compare her with your previous nanny; use
your experience to spot the possible problem areas sooner and
deal with them straight away.

Give her a chance to establish a relationship with the
children, who may be feeling strange at the change, possibly
missing the security of their old nanny and her way of doing
things. If you are around for a few days, try and create long

periods where she is on her own with them but they know that you are not too far away. If you cannot be around you will help your new nanny if you can leave her with as much information as possible, particularly with regard to what the children are and are not allowed to do, what they should and should not eat, and their routine in general. She may need the authority which this information gives her to cope with any cries of 'Mummy lets me' or 'My other nanny let me'. In the first few days she has to balance establishing her authority with making friends with the children; if she is unsure of the boundaries in your household, she will find it difficult.

'Daddy says we can always buy a NEW nanny, so THERE!'

Do not assume that she will know what you want and how you want it done; she may be nervous to start with and the children may play her up. It is particularly important to allow time to talk to her at the end of the day in the early days so that she can tell you how she is getting on and you can give her your support, sorting out any problems as they arise. This is easier to do in the early days than later on, when habits may have been formed.

See also: First Job, First Nanny, Leaving, Overlapping, Previous Nannies

Older Children

 If you choose to employ a nanny to look after your older children you will need one who is able to handle the problems that an older child brings, for example, homework, exam stress, discipline, relationship with peers, independence, sex, drugs and smoking. Since most nannies' training stops at the age of seven you will be relying more on her personality and experience than on qualifications and may find another mother with older children more appropriate for the job.

Before taking a job which involves caring for older children, bear in mind that, whilst this requires the same skills as looking after younger children, you will need the confidence, maturity and ability to apply those skills in the appropriate manner if you are to cope effectively. You will also need to be able to think of activities to suit them.

If you are only a few years older than the older child, you may find it hard to have authority over him or her; their respect will not be won so easily as that of a younger child; they may find it harder to accept you as the new nanny although they will have a better understanding of why you are there.

See also: Extra Children, Questions, Type of Job

Dr David Bennet, *Growing Pains* (Thorsons).
What to do when your children turn into teenagers.

Lynda Madaras, *What's Happening to my Body?*
(Penguin).
A growing-up guide for parents and their daughters.

Alicia Gracia De Lynam, *Stop Copying Me*,
(Hutchinson).
The older brother hates his little sister copying him.
Helpful to explain why.

Siv Widerberg, *The Big Sister* (R & S Books).
Coping with being the eldest.

One-Parent Families

As a nanny you may well be in the position of working for a parent who is bringing up children single-handed – either by choice or circumstance. If you are, you should be aware of the extra responsibility there may be in that job.

Ask yourself:

- Are there any extra duties for you because the family consists of one parent? With only one person available to relieve you you may find your hours are longer than in a two-parent family.
- Are you likely to get too involved with the family and not be able to have a life of your own?
- Are you prepared and able to cope with any emotional problems the children or parent may have as a result of the lack of a parent or partner?
- Can you cope with supporting the parent with his or her feelings and hopes and fears if you need to?
- Does the parent you are working for have a new partner? Will this affect your job? Can you get along with him or her? Are you expected to work for him or her too?

If you take a job with a one-parent family you will need to discuss with your employer how to handle any questions the children may ask about their situation.

As a single parent it is more important than ever that you employ someone that you can get on with and feel comfortable with in your home. You will rely on your nanny more than if you have a partner to share the care of your child; you will probably get closer to her as a result, becoming more of a friend than an employer. She will need to be mature enough to cope with ex-husbands and boyfriends, and committed enough to give the children security.

Since the relationship is likely to be a close one, the nanny will be in the position of being able to take advantage of you more easily than if there are two of you employing her; you will need to be aware of this possibility and work at keeping a healthy respect in the relationship.

See also: Divorce, Questions, Stepchildren

Gingerbread and Community Education Development Centre, *Just Me and the Kids* (Bedford Square Press).
A positive guide to lone parenting; shares experiences, offers advice and gives further help, books and telephone numbers.

Diana Devonport, *One-Parent Families* (Sheldon).
A practical guide to coping.

Felicity Sen and Barry Wilkinson, *My Family* (Bodley Head).
The story of a one-parent family.

Louis Baum, *Are We Nearly There?* (Bodley Head).
One father's day out with child.

Gingerbread Association for One-Parent Families,
35 Wellington Street,
London WC2
Tel: 071 240 0953

National Council for One-Parent Families
255 Kentish Town Road,
London NW5
Tel: 071 267 1361

Only Child

Nannying for an only child has the advantage of being less demanding both physically and mentally, since you can give the child your undivided attention when he or she needs it and only have him or her to think of when you are planning your day. However, you will need to consider the following:

- The job can become boring, especially if the child goes to playgroup or sleeps during the day.
- The parents of an only child tend to be more protective than parents of two or more children. For example they may be fussy over what the child eats or unduly worried about his health, and you may have to constantly reassure them.
- An only child will depend solely on you for company unless you make sure that he has chances to mix with other children. You will have to make more effort to establish a social life for the child.
- He will need extra help with preparation for the arrival of a new baby.

A nanny can be an advantage for an only child. Whereas if you were at home with your child you might spend a lot of time working round the house — since it is your house and garden — your nanny is free of those responsibilities and can concentrate solely on the child. Since most nannies like to socialise, your child will probably come

into contact with more children and become better able to relate to them.

She also acts as another close contact for the child, thus reducing his dependence on you and extending his ability to relate to other adults.

Some mothers fear that the nanny will take their place in the child's affections since he has a one-to-one relationship with her for a large part of the day; if you do feel jealous of your nanny, be wary of letting this affect your relationship with her. She is doing a job, you are the natural mother, and your children know this.

Outings

If you are particularly keen on taking the children on outings it is as well to confirm with your prospective employers at the interview that they are happy for you to do so.

When planning outings check details including opening times, cost and suitability, (particularly if there is a large gap in the ages of the children). Work out the amount of money you will need and clear this with your employer.

SAFETY:

- Never leave the children unattended in a public place.
- Teach them to be aware of the dangers of cars and roads.
- Do not leave the children in the car if you are going out of sight.
- Be aware of the possible danger of strangers.

After the outing report back to the parents; if it went well, you will increase the parents' trust and confidence in you and they will be happy for you to go on future outings.

Quick Tip: Do not go on too many special outings — they will lose their appeal.

Tom had been trying hard to remember to wee in his bright red plastic potty. So it was quite a test when we took him to the local library without a nappy for the first time. All was going well until, while I was talking to his older brother, we heard laughing; we turned round to see Tom confidently weeing into an overturned bright red plastic chair.

 Outings can be fun for both children and nanny, particularly if more than one family go; if you can afford it, encourage your nanny to take the children out, once you are happy that she is able to cope with them. If you are not sure about this, suggest that she goes with a known nanny friend, perhaps one who is more experienced to start with.

It is as well to check where she is going, how she plans to get there, what time she will be coming home, and to ask her to telephone you if she is going to be home later than planned. Give her enough money to cover emergencies. Be sure to find out what they did when they come back and talk to the children about their day; you will then get an idea of whether it was worthwhile.

 Quick Tip: A baby bag, kept stocked up at all times by both mother and nanny, makes going out with a baby/child a simple operation.

See also: Cars, Group Activities, Safety

 Paul Rogers, *Me and Alice Go to the Gallery*, (Bodley Head).
They think the visit will be boring.

Sophie Davies and Diana Bentley, *My Visit to the Museum* (Wayland).
Jonathan visits two museums.

Betty Jerman, *Kids' Britain* (Pan).
Where to go, what to see, and so on.

Elizabeth Holt and Molly Perham, *Kids' London* (Pan).
Comprehensive guide for taking children to London.

Overlapping

Some employers ask the new nanny to start work in the last week of the old nanny's employment, so that she can show her how everything works, where things are, routes to school, introduce her to other nannies, mothers, and so on.

Others consider overlapping to be counterproductive, with the new nanny acquiring all the faults and dodges of the old one and not coming to the job clean. Whether or not overlapping is a good idea obviously depends on the individual nanny, her personality and the circumstances. If the outgoing nanny is leaving under a cloud she might put the new one off the job; if she is leaving happily then she may enthuse the new one. Or they might simply not get on and end up confusing the children. If you have the choice, you will need to consider all these things and the expense before deciding on an overlapping period.

If there is to be an overlapping period it is best to keep it short; it can be difficult for the outgoing nanny to hand over the reins to a new one and difficult for the new nanny to follow in the footsteps of the old, since she will probably want to do things her way regardless. It usually only takes a day to familiarise a new nanny with the running of the household, and if the two nannies do not get on they will not have to put up with each other for long.

If you are able to show your nanny what to do yourself, she will understand what you want right from the start. It also gives you a chance to re-establish how you want things done if things have gone off course with your previous nanny.

The overlapping period can be very hard for both nannies, since both will want to do things their own way, and establishing who is in charge during this time can be difficult. However it can be very useful for learning the practical aspects of the job, and if things go well the incoming nanny will start the job with confidence, while the outgoing

The Old Nanny drops in on the New Nanny.

nanny will feel happier leaving the children with their new carer.

If you are the new nanny you can take advantage of the overlapping period to find out all about the job in greater detail from the existing nanny, which may be easier than asking your new employer. You will want to find out the practicalities, for example, routine (including the weekends), routes to school and shops, car runs, appliances, layout of the house, and names and telephone numbers. Also find out about the things which apply to the children, for example, likes and dislikes, what words the children use, discipline, diet and any particular problems. Watch how the nanny handles situations with both the children and parents and you will learn a lot.

Even if you dislike the nanny, be diplomatic; she knows more about the job than you do and until she has gone it is a good idea to do things her way. The children will be very confused and upset if they sense conflict between you and receive different instructions from each of you. Do not try to take the children away from her or be upset if they want her all the time; this is only natural.

OUTGOING NANNY: If you are the outgoing nanny and have been asked to overlap with the new nanny you will have to cope with mixed emotions. You will be relieved the family has found a replacement for you as this makes leaving easier but you will still feel guilty for doing so.

Most nannies hope the new nanny will keep the same routine and have the same values as they have; this is obviously not always the case. Although you want to leave, the thought of someone else putting the children to bed or telling them off can be very painful.

In spite of your feelings you will need to handle the situation professionally and be sympathetic to the new nanny's feelings. Do not try and influence her into doing things totally your way; she will have discussed with the parents what they want and will be using their instructions as her guide too.

Use the time to help her by showing her the practicalities of the job, answering questions and introducing her to friends. However, do not expect her to be necessarily as friendly with them as you were. It is very tempting to moan to her about the bad side of the job and gossip about the family and neighbours; what you did not like she may not mind, and your negative comments will be offputting and worrying when she is about to have a fresh start in a new or even first job.

One outgoing nanny was showing the new nanny around and telling her about the people in the area. 'The butcher's wife is a gossip, her children are badly behaved and the house is a tip.' The new nanny smiled. 'I know. She's my cousin.'

If you can be friends with her and help each other, your last days in the job will be much happier and you will feel more able to come back to visit the family while she is there.

See also: First Job, Leaving, New Job / New Nanny, Previous Nannies, Social Life

---

Parties

 Mothers with nannies are undoubtedly fortunate when it comes to parties; nannies are usually more experienced at children's parties than you, good at organising them and often enjoy doing it. Their job gives them plenty of experience of organising a number of small children at a time and so they are not fazed by the thought of coping with a party; many mothers fear this annual event and pay a small fortune to hand the responsibility to someone else.

Your nanny will also be invaluable at knowing the names of the children and their parents which you as a working mum may be unsure of and embarrassed about.

Although it may mean asking her to work on her day off, do not be shy of asking for your nanny's help — some take pride in their party-organising ability and may even be offended if you do not involve them; you can perhaps give them time off to make up for the party.

Most nannies are asked to help at or to organise the children's parties. You should be willing to help out during work time with the preparation but may face a dilemma if the party is to be held during a day that you do not normally work. You will have to decide between volunteering or negotiating payment or time off in lieu. Many nannies choose to be there regardless.

Quick Tip: It is helpful to notice and keep a record of any good ideas for children's parties for when you need them.

Discuss your party plans with your employers including:

– Type of party (birthday, Christmas, fancy dress, games,

entertainer, outing).
- How many guests to attend (children, relatives and helpers).
- Time and place.
- Food, party prizes, decorations and leaving bags.
- Cost.

Your employers may want your advice on presents for the child, as you will have seen them play with other children's toys and heard their requests more often.

One of your duties may be to organise a birthday present and card for your charge to take to a party. Check with your employer first, as they may like to do this; but if not, ask how much you should spend.

Juliet Bawden, *Crazy Presents* (Hutchinson).
How to make unusual presents.

Jane Asher's Children's Parties (Pelham).
Comprehensive guide to parties for children aged nought—twelve years.

Chris Powling and Scoular Anderson, *Harry's Party* (Young Lions).
Harry wrecks other children's parties, until he has his own.

Angela Hollest, *Parties for Older Children* (Piatkus).
Party ideas, games and food suitable for an older age group.

Anne Civardi and Stephen Cartwright, *Going to a Party: First Experiences*.
Suitable for under-fives.

Pets

If you want your nanny to care for your bad-tempered cat, pedigree bitch on heat, highly-strung stallion and pet viper with a delicate stomach, then you must make this clear in the interview, since pets are not part of a nanny's training / job. It may not seem much to ask her to 'feed the cat', and she will probably be happy to do it, but if she is asked to take fuller responsibility she may feel put upon, justifiably so if you have not clarified her position before she takes the job. Also make sure you have the right equipment for transporting pets to the vet.

If you are allergic to animals DON'T TAKE THE JOB! You won't be able to avoid the pet and your allergic reaction may make caring for the children difficult.

If there is a pet in the family:

- Keep food bowls and litter trays out of reach.
- Clear up poo, wee and sick immediately. You may feel this is not your job — for the health and safety of the children, it is!
- You may have to clean out hutches and beds, since the novelty of caring for an animal soon wears off for a child.

Children, particularly toddlers, are often cruel to pets; it is important to teach them the right way to handle their pet to avoid both child and pet getting hurt.

When a pet dies it can be very traumatic for a child. It is possibly his or her first experience of death. It may help the child to see the pet (if in a suitable condition) to say goodbye. Be prepared to answer the child's questions both immediately and for a while afterwards. When a pet dies, if possible ring your employer to let her know what has happened so she is prepared for what she may come home to.

In my second job we had a pet hamster — no bother and quite pleasant until he decided to hibernate — or did he? Once the children were at school I took Freddie to the vet, where he was pronounced well and truly D-E-A-D. I rang the mother to tell her, in case the children were upset. She was in a board meeting so I left the message that I was 'very sorry, but Freddie had died'. Her secretary got a stiff drink, some cigarettes and a sympathetic colleague to stand by, and steeled herself for a difficult half hour. Jane was called out of her board meeting and gently sat down, given the drink and a cigarette and the news — Freddie's dead. Jane got up and said, 'Oh dear' and went back into the meeting, leaving one stunned secretary.

See also: Contract, Duties, Interviews

 RSPCA Pet Guides, *Care For Your Dog* (Collins).
Many different animals also covered in this series.

Nigel Snell, *Sam's Rabbit*, *Nina's Gerbil*, *Emma's Kitten*
(Hodder and Stoughton).
A first care book.

Pregnancy

A nanny is not entitled to any maternity rights from her
employer, unless that employer employs five or more people
including herself. Therefore unlike other jobs, a nannying job
does not have to be kept open for the nanny to return to after the
child is born, nor will she qualify for paid maternity leave
(SMP) from her employer. However, if the nanny has paid
National Insurance Contributions, she will qualify for Statutory
Maternity Allowance (SMA). If this is the case she should
contact the DSS when she becomes pregnant who will advise
her on Statutory Maternity Allowance which is payable for a
total of eighteen weeks, from eleven to fourteen weeks before
the expected date of confinement.

When you are pregnant and happy to be so you will
have to discuss with your employer how this will affect
your job. How and when you tell her will depend on
your relationship with each other, what you think her attitude
may be and the circumstances under which you are pregnant.

Some employers will be pleased for you and help all they can,
allowing you to carry on working for them until you have to
leave. You will need to agree a leaving date which will be subject
to your state of health and expected date of confinement.

Others may not react favourably towards your news; they
may feel that you will not be able to cope properly with your job

and your pregnancy and it is possible that you will not. Be prepared for this reaction, think through your plans, and decide what you will do if you are asked to leave before you want to.

If you have been in your job for more than two years your employer is not legally allowed to dismiss you for being pregnant unless she can prove that your pregnancy is affecting your duties. If she does dismiss you for being pregnant, the dismissal is unfair.

If your job and circumstances allow, you may be able to successfully carry on working throughout your pregnancy and stay with the family after the birth of your child.

If your nanny announces she is pregnant, whilst you will obviously be pleased for her if that is what she wants, you may well feel dismayed since in the long run this will probably mean finding a new nanny and the associated unwanted upheaval. However, if you like her and want to keep her – in the short or long term – you will need to support her. If she wants to stay with you and carry on working for you until she has the baby you will need to decide whether or not you think she can cope with your children adequately whilst coping with her pregnancy.

You may consider continuing to employ her after she has had the baby. If so, ask yourself:

- What effect will this have on your family, household and relationships?
- Will she cope with her baby and her job?
- Will your children cope with the arrival of her baby?
- If she lives in, is your house big enough?
- Will she change her mind once the baby is born?
- Can you arrange cover for her while she has the baby and when the baby is sick?

When your employer tells you she is pregnant you may have mixed emotions – whilst you will obviously be happy for her it will mean a radical change to your job which you may or may not welcome.

As the nanny, you will be able to help the mother during the pregnancy by offering her support and helping out where you can. It is one of those times when, as long as you are not being taken for granted, you should not mind doing that bit extra.

 If you become pregnant you will need to discuss all the implications of this situation with your nanny, including:

- How her job will change; more responsibility, more work, hours and wages.
- The effect of the new arrival on the other children; how you and your nanny will prepare them for it.
- Your maternity leave — how this will affect her routine and how you will work together.

ABORTION

If you are pregnant and not happy about the prospect as you had not planned on having a baby at that time, you may be in a state of shock and disbelief. You will want to think very carefully indeed about the implications of having the baby or terminating the pregnancy. Talking to a close friend or parent (if possible) or discussing it with your doctor will help. It will depend on your relationship with your employers as to whether or not you want to involve them at this stage over the decision.

If you do decide to terminate your pregnancy you may have to tell your employer. It may be best just to talk to the mother. Her reaction will depend on her own religious / ethical point of view, and on how it affects her as well as you. She may be cross and upset or concerned and helpful — or all of these! Find out if the termination will affect your job in any way.

Try and arrange a time for the operation that will cause least disruption to your job, for example, a Friday. You will probably need a minimum of three days' rest before you go back to work, although much depends on your mental attitude and state of mind. It is not unusual to be given a week off, in which case perhaps a nanny friend could cover for you. Do not involve the children; if you need to explain your absence, a small white lie is sufficient.

If your employer has an abortion treat the knowledge with the strictest confidentiality.

 You may find you are in the situation of knowing that your nanny is planning an abortion without being told about it. Unless your nanny wants your help you will do best not to get involved. If she does want you to help, she will need your understanding and support; point her in the direction of her doctor or the local family planning clinic and let her decide what to do about it. Or as some employers do, you could help arrange and pay for it.

If you yourself need an abortion be wary of confiding in your nanny; you are employing her, and whilst the temptation to tell her may be strong if you get on well with her, it may be more difficult to maintain a healthy employee / employer relationship having discussed such a personal subject.

See also: Babies, Illness, Questions

Angela Phillips and Jill Rakusen, *Our Bodies Ourselves* (Penguin).
Has good chapters on birth control, abortion and pregnancy.

The British Pregnancy Advisory Service,
Austy Manor,
Wootton Wawen,
Solihull,
West Midlands B95 6BX
Tel: 0564 793225
Offers support, advice and counselling. Contact the head office for your local branch.

The Pregnancy Advisory Service,
11–13 Charlotte Street,
London W1P 1HD
Tel: 071 637 8962
Information and support on all aspects of pregnancy.

Brook Advisory Centre,
153a East Street,
London SE17 2SD
Tel: 071 708 1234 (Central Office)
     071 708 1390
Information and support on all aspects of pregnancy.

Previous Nannies

You may stay in contact with all your old nannies or none of them; whatever the situation, always give the new nanny a chance to establish herself with the children before inviting the old one back to visit; it is not fair on the children or the new nanny to confuse the line of authority in the first days. Some employers make the mistake of assuming that their old nanny will get on well with the new one; whilst they may do so, do not underestimate possible rivalry between them, and be aware that they may simply dislike each other intensely.

Unless you are the family's first nanny, at some time during your job you are likely to meet one of their previous nannies. When you know this is going to happen you may have some doubts about it. Will you like her? Are you as good as she was? How will she behave towards you? How will the children and parents react?

When she does visit be prepared for the children to show her a lot of affection and do not be hurt by this. It is tempting but unnecessary to prove to her how well you are doing with the children / family / home.

Some nannies will come back and try and take over — should she go too far you will have to politely remind her that you are now in charge. If this does not do the trick and she visits a lot you may have to ask the parents for support.

If you go back to visit your previous family:

- Leave a suitable time gap.
- Always ring first and ask the parents if it is appropriate for you to visit.
- It may be better in the first instance to go when the new nanny is not on duty.
- Be prepared for the children to be different.
- Be prepared for the new nanny to have changed the way things are done.
- Do not offer advice unless asked.
- Do not go back with your new charges for a while. Give the children a few months to adjust to their new nanny.

One previous nanny asked the new one what she was getting the two-year-old for his birthday. She was told a posting box and that the child would have it after his birthday party. The previous nanny came to the party with a deluxe posting box which the child loved, leaving the new nanny with a useless present and — if she complained — a tricky situation.

See also: First Job, First Nanny, New Job / New Nanny, Overlapping

Privacy

The loss of privacy is one of the biggest adjustments you will make when you take on a nanny; sharing your home with a third person whom you would not choose to share it with in any other circumstance is not always easy.

You may tend to overlook the fact that your nanny may also suffer from lack of privacy herself when she lives in. To help both you and her you can:

- Have a specific area in the house which is yours only.
- Have specific times of the day when she knows she should not join you.
- Establish between you that privacy is important to you and that there will be occasions when you will ask her to leave you alone as a family; explain that she is not to take this personally.
- Establish at the interview whether or not you would like her to be in the house at weekends; make sure she has somewhere to go if you want the house to yourself.
- Choose an independent nanny who has a busy social life.
- Whenever an event which is out of the usual run, for example a party, is planned, make it clear whether or not she is invited and under what terms — on or off duty.
- Do not go into her room without knocking, or unless invited.
- Tell her in advance if you are going to be out and what times you think you will be home.
- Put locks on doors of bathrooms and loos.

Privacy can be difficult if you are working as a live-in nanny. You will probably be used to having some time and space to yourself at home and may find adjusting to the constraints of living in someone else's house somewhat bewildering at first.

Your attitude and the signals you give your employers and charges will show them how much privacy you want. If you immediately go to your room every night when they come home and do not go out again until next morning, you can reasonably expect to be left alone. However if you always leave your door open, join the family for supper and drinks, they may well assume that privacy is less important to you. A happy medium is best — be part of the family but have some periods of time on your own to have a break from them and give them a break from you.

The house and more importantly your accommodation will contribute to how much privacy you get and give. A large house with a bathroom to yourseif and bedroom on a different level obviously makes it more private; you will need to bear this in mind when you are shown round the house at the interview. If you require a lock on your bedroom or bathroom door do not be afraid to ask for one. There is nothing worse than having to escape to the toilet to read a letter from your boyfriend and to have to hold the door shut with one foot and keep your balance with the other!

Do not overlook the fact that your employers and their family also require privacy; how much will vary from job to job and depend largely on your hours, social life and the family's routine. No matter how well you like and get on with each other be careful not to be over-friendly and assume you have the right always to be around. Knowing when to be with the family and when to disappear is not always obvious. Hopefully they will make it easy for you and give you clear guidelines, particularly in the early days, but if they do not you will have to read the signs to judge when you are welcome and when you are not. If in doubt ask if they are happy for you to be there and offer to go if necessary.

See also: Bathrooms, Bedrooms, Boyfriends, Guests, Interviews, Social Life, Weekends

---

Questions

Who is God?
Why do people die?
How are babies made?
Why are strangers dangerous?
What is AIDS?
Why haven't I got a daddy?
Why do people fight wars?

As parents our upbringing, beliefs, education and experience all contribute to the way we answer our children's questions. Since you cannot assume that your nanny's attitudes and beliefs will necessarily be the same as yours, you need to make sure she is aware of what *you* want your children to know and believe, and how you go about answering their questions.

If she becomes embarrassed or unsure when the children ask questions, or even evades answering them, they will sense her awkwardness, be reluctant to ask again and maybe worry about it. If you want to be sure that your children are given information on a particular subject in the way you want, you may prefer to initiate the discussion with them yourself — in which case your nanny should know what you have said.

There will be times when the children will ask you difficult questions which will require careful answering — they may be connected to family situations or to outside influences such as world events and the environment. The answers you give should reflect the parents' views and wishes, which may not necessarily be your own.

It is helpful if you have discussed sensitive areas with your employers and have found out what the children already know. If the children then ask you new questions remember to tell your employers how you answered them; the parents can then be consistent if they are asked the same questions later.

Books are a good way to help you answer children's questions; make sure the book is suitable for the child's age and covers the subject in an appropriate way. Go through the book with the child to make sure he understands it.

 Quick Tip: Always attempt to answer the question; if you do not know, say so and find out together.

See also: Adoption, Bereavement, Child Development, Communication, Divorce, Leaving, Older Children, One-Parent Families, Pregnancy, Stepchildren

 Sheila and Celia Kitzinger, *Talking with Children about Things that Matter* (Pandora).
Includes chapters on wars, AIDS, sex and death.

Claire Rayner, *The Body Book* (Piccolo).
Explains with simple text and illustrations how the body works.

David Macauley, *The Way Things Work* (Dorling Kindersley).
An extensively illustrated fun guide.

Routine

 A flexible but well-structured routine is essential if the nanny is to manage her job well and the children are to be happy. The nanny who gets the chores out of the way first thing in the morning, and who stops the children's activities in good time so that she can get them to bed without a rush, will create a more relaxed environment. It makes a great deal of difference to the end of your day if the house is calm and organised when you walk in and you do not have to deal with chaos.

– Find out at the interview if the nanny is organised and efficient by asking her questions about the sort of routine she has, or thinks she might have in your household. If it is her first job and she is unused to handling a household you will have to be prepared to help her establish a routine.

You may want to leave the entire planning of your children's lives to your nanny, including visits to dentist, clinics, cub camps, and music teachers. Or you may prefer to keep control over these things and just delegate the daily care to your nanny, in close consultation with her. Either way good communication is essential.

Quick Tip: If you have any long-term plans for the family your nanny needs to know in good time.

Your routine is often crucial to the smooth running of the household; being organised says a lot about you and your attitude to the job. It gives the adults and, more importantly, the children around you a feeling of trust and security. It will also give you more free time in the long run.

You will be affected by the existing organisation in your employers' household, so at the interview find out about the routine the family (and the nanny) already have and decide if you can fit in.

All the areas of your job have to be organised both daily and weekly, in line with the parents' routine:

- Activities: at home and outside, with friends and on your own.
- Beds and bedrooms: cleaning and changing.
- Bedtime: bath, teeth, book.
- Clothes: washing, drying, ironing, mending, putting away.
- Doctors, dentists, hairdressers, clinics.
- Driving: school runs, runs to friends and other activities.
- Meals: shopping, cooking, clearing up.
- School, playgroup, mother and toddler.
- Sleeps: if children are young enough.
- Social visits: yours and the children's.
- Toys: tidying, repairing, keeping clean.
- Any other job particular to that household, for example, the parents' ironing, walking the dog.

Having identified these areas in your particular job, you can then decide how best to structure your day and week in the number of hours available to you.

1. Plan ahead — both daily and weekly, discussing forthcoming events with your employers.
2. Allow yourself more than enough time for each task; if something goes wrong you will have time to deal with it and if all goes well you will have some free time.
3. Pace yourself knowing your own limitations.
4. Do not do too much at first but gradually build things up.
5. Get the boring jobs out of the way first thing in the morning.
6. Be flexible — have alternatives worked out in case of unforeseen circumstances.
7. Have everything done by the end of the day/week.

'No, everything's FINE. Just a TEENY problem with the washing machine'.

At times you will need to plan a long way ahead, maybe arranging activities for the school holidays, planning special events or visits to relatives. If you do, make sure you keep a record of them maybe on the family's calendar — if you were ever ill or away it would be easier for someone else to cover for you.

See also: Duties, Interview, Weekends

Safety

Give your nanny strict instructions as to how you want your children and your house looked after and be sure that they are followed.

Do not take her knowledge of safety for granted — prevention is best. Discuss the possible danger areas round the house, garden and outside the home, including: dangerous and poisonous substances, electricity cables and sockets, other kitchen hazards — knives, utensils, saucepan handles, stoves — bathroom hazards, fires, poisonous plants and berries, ponds and wells, dog mess, cars and roads, strangers.

It is a good idea to check occasionally that the standards you have asked for are being maintained. If your nanny does not take your safety instructions seriously you will lose your trust and confidence in her. Not taking suitable safety precautions can be a sackable offence and if you discover that she is cutting corners, you must deal with it straight away.

As the children's nanny you are responsible for their safety at all times. You should be aware of all the possible dangers they may face and safeguard against each accordingly.

You will find that each family you work for will have a different attitude to safety. Some are very concerned and take every precaution while others may be more relaxed about it. In either case, since you are responsible when your employers are not there, *you* should be happy with the safety measures in the environment you are being asked to work in. If you are not, because you feel some areas are dangerous, you will have to approach your employers about improving them. Simply telling the parents of your concerns may be enough or you may have to ask for specific things, for example fitting locks on cupboards and putting plug caps into sockets.

You may have the opposite problem where the parents worry constantly about safety and this may make it difficult for you to work normally. If your employers are over-fussy it may be that they need to get to know you better and trust you. For this to happen you will have to build up their confidence in you. This may be done by:

- Not giving them any reason to have this concern.
- Showing them through words and actions that you understand safety.
- Make a point of telling them how you keep their child safe, particularly on outings.
- If you are visiting friends, reassure your employers that you will still be safety-conscious.

If you ever have to leave the house empty at any time of the day you must make sure you have left it safe. This includes locking it up securely, (make sure you know how to use all the security locks), checking that fires are off or out, that water is off, and that any appliances left on are working correctly.

If a fire or burglary happens while you are in charge, you will feel guilty even if it was not your fault, but at least you will have a clear conscience if you took the usual safety measures.

If you discover a burglary:

- Protect the children. Ask someone else to look after them if possible.
- Telephone the local police.
- Do not touch anything.
- Contact your employers; they will probably want to come home straight away.
- While you wait, look to see what is missing.

See also: Accidents, Callers, Cars, Outings

Jane Tye and Tim Challis, *Safety First* (Dent paperbacks).
Written with the British Safety Council. Has first aid and safety number guide. How to avoid accidents and what to do when they do happen.

Series 819, *Road Sense, First Steps in First Aid, Home Safety, Water Safety* (Ladybird).

Dorothy Baldwin and Claire Lister, *Safety When Alone* (Wayland).
One of a series of safety books for children aged five and over.

The Child Accident Prevention Trust,
28 Portland Place,
London W1N 4DE
Tel: 071 636 2545

Schools

As a working mother you are at a disadvantage if you are concerned to have a close relationship with your children's schools and nurseries. If your child is happy at school this may not be a problem, but if he is having difficulties which need sorting out you will find it frustrating and worrying not being on the spot to help. Because you are not there:

- You cannot just pop in to have a word with the teacher, or help out with the reading or the playgroup duty.
- You will not be known at the school gate by the other mums and may therefore find it hard to be accepted by them.
- You may not be there when your child comes home from school when the day's events are still fresh in his or her mind, and you may therefore not have intimate know-

ledge of activities and relationships or be able to help with homework.
- The teacher/other mums may frown on you quietly for working and delegating your children to your nanny.

However, if you have a good nanny she can help with all these problems, making a relationship with your child's teacher and with the other mums. The 'mother mafia' can be daunting and she will need to be persistent and not be expected to be accepted by all of them. She will also need your authority behind her. Have a word with the teacher and tell her about your nanny; if possible, have them meet with you there. If the teacher sees that you trust your nanny she will do so too. Your nanny can also be briefed to keep an eye on school and school work and help your child if he is having difficulties. However, never let your nanny end up as piggy in the middle; if you do get involved temporarily with the teachers and she has been acting on your behalf previously, she must be told what has been said so that she can continue to liaise efficiently.

You may find it useful to join the Parent-Teacher Association or similar and make an effort to get to know other parents in the evenings.

CAR RUNS: If you or your nanny have the option of sharing the burden of taking and collecting the children from school, you will want to satisfy yourself that the cars your children will travel in have the correct safety equipment and that this will be used. This being so, and you are happy about the other drivers, you will save on petrol money and have a back-up system in case of emergencies. The only disadvantage is that your nanny will have less contact with the school or playgroup as a result and your child will not always have his own chauffeur.

Most nannying jobs involve caring for at least one child who goes to a school, nursery or playgroup. The days and times of attendance will greatly influence the routine in your job. Always ask at the interview where the children go to school, how many days they attend, if you have to help there at any time, for example, on duty at the playgroup, and whether or not you will be part of a car run.

When you are at any one of these places with the children, remember you are representing their parents. You will be the one who sees how happy the children are going in and out of the establishment; you will see what work they are doing and how well they are getting on; and you will meet the other children and mothers. Make sure you inform the parents of everything that is going on and act as the go-between if necessary. You may need to attend school events if the parents cannot go; or you may want to go but not be invited (especially if you are off duty) — if this is the case, do not be afraid to ask.

In some circumstances the teachers may approach you first over a problem the child may have; should this happen, or if you think one of the children has a problem, always discuss this with the parents first to see what action they want to take. Whilst some parents will be pleased that the problem is identified, others may not want to recognise it; either way, it is for them to decide how they want to approach it.

One of your duties may be to oversee homework and holiday projects. Help the children by getting into a routine that allows time and space for doing these tasks. You may also be asked to get costumes ready for the school play or collect boxes for the junk modelling table.

 Quick Tip: Remember to show the parents the children's good work.

When children start a new school / nursery / playgroup you can help to prepare them by talking to them, taking them to see it, and if appropriate staying with them for a few sessions.

You will also have to make new friends and be accepted by a new social circle; this is not always a very easy or pleasant experience but it is worth the effort, since once you have done it you will be able to share car runs, teas and outings and life will be more pleasant for both you and the children.

See also: Cars, Child Development, Communication

 Janet and Allan Ahlberg *Starting School* (Viking / Kestrel).

Fiona Pragoff, *I Go to Nursery School* (Magnet).
What happens at Stacey's nursery school.

Helen Oxenbury, *Playschool* (Walker).
First picture books for under-fives.

Margaret Joy, *You're in the Juniors Now* (Faber).
Changing from infants to juniors, twelve stories covering the school year.

Margaret Basham, *Getting Ready for School* (Longman).
A parents' guide. Advice on preparation and settling in.

Shopping

Shopping for the family may be one of your duties; the amount varies from family to family. Some ask you to do everything while others ask you to get just what you and the children need. It can be an advantage to do the shopping, as you will have the chance to buy exactly what you want for the coming week for yourself and the children.

Before you embark on the first shopping trip briefly discuss with your employer:

- What she wants you to get.
- How much she expects you to spend.
- How you will pay.
- When and where she wants you to shop.
- If she has any particular food preferences.

If you ask your nanny to shop as part of her duties be aware that her attitude to food may well be different to yours; if you have a specific requirement, for instance, avoidance of E numbers, you will need to be clear about it.

Your nanny should not take your child on endless shopping trips for herself; most children hate shopping and your nanny is not paid to take them, except where you have asked her to buy something for them. However, since nannies do not have an official lunch hour, it is only reasonable to allow her to do her own shopping now and then if the children are elsewhere or if she is out shopping for the family.

See also: Clothes, Costs, Duties

John Burningham, *The Shopping Basket* (Jonathan Cape). A shopping errand becomes a battle of wits.

Pam Zinnemann-Hope, *Let's Go Shopping*, *Ned* (Walker). Chaos when Ned and Fred the dog go shopping with Dad.

Social Life

After terms and conditions, your social life is probably the most important factor in helping you to be happy in your job. If you are the kind of person that enjoys going out most evenings and inviting friends around both when you are on and off duty, you will need to make sure at the interview that your prospective employers and the duties of the job will allow this to happen.

Moving to a new area and making friends can be quite daunting and for a while you are bound to feel homesick and lonely. Be brave. There are several ways to meet people, including:

- Joining a club.
- Taking evening classes.
- Going along to a mother and toddler group or other activity group. Find out about these in the library and local papers.
- Asking the agency (if you used one) to tell you of other nannies they have placed in that area. Some run their own friendship clubs.
- Asking neighbours, mothers, schools and playgroups if they know any other nannies.
- Looking in the personal columns of *Nursery World* for nanny friendship groups or nannies advertising themselves.
- Advertising yourself in the local shops, newspapers, or *Nursery World*. Ask your employer first — be careful what you say in adverts for security reasons.

NANNY, NEW TO PUTNEY, WOULD
LIKE TO MEET OTHER NANNIES.
PLEASE TELEPHONE 000 111 2222.

 Quick Tip: Ask your friends to write to you — letters lessen loneliness.

There may be a 'nanny network' already set up that the parents or the previous nanny know about and can introduce you to. This can work well unless you find that you do not fit in with the previous nanny's circle of contacts. It can also be hard to be accepted in a group that already know each other well, have a routine and may be missing the previous nanny. Take your time to become part of that group and be careful what you say about the family, the previous nanny and the terms and conditions you are working under. Learn what you can from them about the area. If all else fails, start again and gradually build up your own circle of friends.

Nannying is unusual from the point of view that some of your social life happens while you are on duty — lunches, teas, outings and night stays with your nanny friends and their charges. This is full of advantages for all. However:

Do:
- Make sure at all times the children are benefitting and happy.
- Give the children some time on their own at home with you.
- Plan other activities with the children.
- Make sure the socialising is not one-sided.
- Inform the parents where you went, what the children did, and if it was successful or not.

Don't:
- Neglect the rest of your duties.
- Overdo it.

– Forget to socialise with your charge's friends who do not
have a nanny. You may become friendly with their
parents or they could come to visit on their own.

You may like to have friends round in the evenings or
occasionally have a dinner party. You will need to discuss this
with your employer and observe her house rules.

If your employers are ignoring your need for a social life you
will need to talk to them about this.

Do not underestimate the importance of your nanny's
social life. A happy nanny is one who is happy with her
social situation, whether it is active or not. You will
need to assess your nanny's potential for loneliness or a social
life at the interview. What sort of social life do you want your
nanny to have? Do you want her to babysit a lot? Is she the sort
who will make friends easily? Is she likely to be homesick? Will
she lean too heavily on you for company or will she be out every
night and too tired to work in the morning? Will she be happy to
stay in and read and watch TV? Has she a boyfriend? Two?
More? The answers to these questions will help you assess how
well your nanny will fit in with your household and routine.

A live-in nanny is in a unique situation — her 'home' life takes
place at her work place and she requires the good will and
permission of her employer in order to entertain friends. Be
reasonable but firm; make the rules clear but respect her need
for social contact.

Her social life is her business, as long as it does not affect you
and your family adversely; how involved you become will
depend on the type of nanny you employ. An outgoing nanny
may need reminding that there is work to do along with the
lunches, teas and nights out, whilst a shy one may need your
encouragement and help to socialise.

One of the most difficult areas with a live-in nanny is the loss
of privacy in your own home; she cannot be expected to
disappear telepathically when you want her to. You need to
make it absolutely clear early on in her employment where and
when and how she is to fit into your social life, if at all. It is

difficult for her if you do not do so and awful for you to spend evenings wishing she was in her room and not sharing your sherry with you and your neighbour (who she may well regard as a friend during the day).

You can help yourself and her by establishing certain rooms or times of day when she is not welcome; if you break this, make it clear that you have done so and for how long. Make her room a welcoming place to go and if possible have a room in the house which is for you and yours only.

See also: Babysitting, Boyfriends, Communication, First Job, First Nanny, Interviews, New Job / New Nanny, Overlapping, Privacy, Weekends

---

Nursery World,
Personal Department,
Child Care Classified,
The Schoolhouse Workshop,
51, Calthorpe Street,
London WC1X 0HH
A fee is charged for your advertisement. They forward the replies to you.

Nannies Need Nannies Association,
28 May Street,
South Shields,
Tyne and Wear NE33 3AJ
Tel: 091 454 2617
A friendship contact service for lonely nannies, formed in 1981. Send a s.a.e. A fee is charged.

The National Association of Certificated Nursery Nurses,
162 Langdale Road,
Thornton Heath,
Surrey CR4 7PR

This association is run by nursery nurses for nursery nurses. Formed in 1948, its aim is to represent nursery nurses and keep them informed by speakers, conferences and newsletters, and so on, on all aspects of training and child care. A fee is charged.

Special Needs

This section covers situations where special knowledge and care are needed in order to look after the child adequately – physically, emotionally and mentally. For example, children who are blind, have Down's Syndrome, muscular dystrophy, epilepsy, are victims of an accident, are gifted, or are hyperactive, need someone special to help them – and so do their parents.

For those looking for care for their child and for those wishing to work with special needs children, the NNEB and other training courses include work with handicapped children – your local college may be able to help you. It is also worthwhile approaching some of the organisations which deal with specific special needs; they may be able to help put nanny and mother in touch with each other, and can offer support to both.

If you have a child with special needs you will obviously have to be even more careful in selecting the nanny you employ to look after him or her. Describe your child's special needs in the advertisement to save wasting time, and bring it up first at the interview. Tell her exactly what needs your child has and what she will be required to do. You may have to be prepared to pay a little more for your nanny – you can ask your local DSS if you qualify for attendance or mobility allowance to help you. You may of course need to employ a nanny with nursing qualifications if your child requires that level of care.

If your child's special needs are not known at the time you employ your nanny but develop during her time with you, both you and she may want to review her employment with you. She may not want to continue to work for you, she may not be qualified to cope, or you may wish to stop working and look after your child.

If you decide to nanny for a child with special needs, you will have to have a full understanding of what is involved and be prepared to cope with whatever his or her requirements are. For this reason it is very important at the interview stage that you are absolutely clear about what you are being asked to take on, and the kind of routine you are likely to have.

You are likely to develop a very close relationship with the family as the situation will require you all to liaise constantly with each other, discussing and agreeing ways of dealing with events. Since the parents will have to cope with their own emotions as well as the child, it will help you and them if you try and keep a professional distance from the problems. You may have to liaise with a doctor or other specialist helper from time to time, learning how to administer medication or therapy.

This type of job may include doing all the normal duties expected from a nanny, as well as the extra ones the condition may bring. You may well be responsible for other children in the family as well and must be able to care for them too, giving them the attention they require and making sure (where possible) that they do not miss out on activities. They will need your help in understanding and tolerating the special needs of their sibling.

You may be the first one to have suspicions about a child having a special need; if so and where you are able, tactfully discuss this with your employers. You may meet with resistance – if you do, a health visitor, teacher or doctor may be able to help.

If a child develops a special need once you have started to work for the family, you will have to help and support the family where you can. When appropriate you will need to discuss and redefine your job with your employer, which will help you to decide whether or not you can cope with the new situation. If you feel you cannot, you will probably feel very guilty about wanting to leave at such a difficult time. However this is a better option than not coping or being unhappy, as ultimately everyone suffers if this is the case.

See also: Agencies

Andrinna McCormack, *Coping with your Handicapped Child* (Chambers).

Sylvia Cassedy, *Me and Morton* (Bodley Head).
A child learns to live with his handicapped sibling.

Nearly every special need has its own organisation; use your telephone book to find the nearest branch to you.

The National Library for the Handicapped Child,
20 Bedford Way,
London WC1
Tel: 071 255 1363
The public can use the books and materials to help handicapped children to read.

Connect
Tel: 0272 290777 Ext. 536
Information and resources service for adults and children with learning difficulties. Including holiday, national organisations, bulletins and workshop information.

Contact a Family
16 Strutton Ground,
London SW1P 2HP
Tel: 071 222 2695 (Head Office)
Puts families with special needs children in touch with each other.

National AIDS Helpline
Tel: 0800 567123
Offers advice on all aspects of AIDS and HIV Positive
conditions.

Terrence Higgins Trust,
52 – 54 Gray's Inn Road,
London WC1X 8JU
Tel: 071 242 1010 (Helpline)
      071 405 2381 (Legal line: Wed 7 pm – 10 pm)
Offers advice and counselling to those with the virus
and their friends and relatives.

Staff

You may work for a family which employs other staff
– usually a cleaner, sometimes a gardener and, more
rarely, a cook, maid, butler, chauffeur or second
nanny. This may well be mentioned in the advertisement, but it
is as well to ask at the interview whether or not any other staff
are employed, and how this will affect you and your job.

During your first days find out:

- What days and times they work. You will need to talk to
  them to plan your routine round them.
- What their job involves.
- If you have to help in any way, for example, clearing up
  before they come.
- What the arrangements are with regard to security and
  payment.

If you are lucky you will have no problems with other staff,
but many nannies do have bad experiences and you may need to
be tolerant and tactful to maintain good relationships.

Possible problem areas with other staff are:

- Confidentiality: you may find you are piggy in the
  middle, being put in an uncomfortable position. For

example, you may find that the number of hours paid for
by your employer are not actually being done by the
cleaner. If you speak up, he / she may lose his / her job; if
you do not and your employer finds out, she may want to
know why you did not tell her sooner.
- The house and contents being abused, for example, the
  telephone being used for long-distance calls, with you
  getting the blame.
- Food being eaten by staff or their children.
- Sexual advances.
- Criticism: they know all about everything and you are
  doing everything 'wrong'.

If you find yourself with any of these problems you will have
to decide where your loyalty lies and speak to your employer if
you can.

 Quick Tip: Do not leave the children in the care of
another member of staff, unless agreed with your
employer.

*Julia was very unhappy in her job, mainly due to her relationship
with Mrs Hughes, the daily cleaning lady, who constantly criticised
her. Julia decided she could not continue to work there and found
herself another job in another part of the town. On her first day the
cleaning lady came; Julia could not believe it — it was Mrs
Hughes.*

 The relationship between nannies and other members
of your staff is not always an easy one. You can help
prevent unnecessary conflict if you:

- Define their jobs clearly so that each knows what the
  other is responsible for. For example, the cleaner may not
  be responsible for keeping the children's rooms clean.
- Make them complain to you and not to each other; ask
  them to deal with you directly if there is a problem with
  the job.

- Avoid getting messages to one via the other.
- Avoid playing them off against each other.
- Treat their gripes about each other with caution.

Since your nanny is at home all day and sees the other staff at work, she will have a true picture of what they do. She will also need to get on with them, and may end up with divided loyalties. You will need to be astute and, if necessary, give your nanny an opening occasionally to talk about other staff members — she may be having to keep secrets which she is not happy about.

Unless it has been agreed at the interview, most nannies do not do any cleaning. However, if you are looking for a cleaner, you may consider offering the job first to the nanny. Although she may not offer to do it, she may prefer to, rather than having a cleaner in the house. If she does agree to take on the cleaning, she will obviously need to be paid for it at a cleaner's rate.

See also: Communication

Stepchildren

In many homes where there is a step-parent and stepchildren the relationships are as satisfactory as those in a natural family and do not present any more or fewer problems. If, however, there are problems a nanny can be a great help since she is outside the family situation and therefore able to offer an unbiased ear if the children need one. She can also help make visiting stepchildren feel welcome and help those she cares for accept the visitors.

If she is to support the children effectively, she will need clear guidelines from you regarding the various relationships between stepchildren and parents, new partners and exisiting children. She should be told all the basic details at the interview so that she knows the situation before taking the job; should it arise

once she is with you, you will need to review the terms and
conditions of her employment with you, particularly if she will
be required to take on more children, either permanently or
periodically.

There are many nannying jobs that involve caring for
stepchildren either living permanently as part of the
family or coming to stay for visits at the weekends or
holidays. You should be told at the interview if this is so. It is
helpful to find out whether or not there have been or still are any
particular difficulties; depending on their ages, children may
well have adapted to their situation, or you may find that they
are having problems with some of the following:

- Emotional insecurity and adjustment to their own situation.
- Accepting the step-parent, or the step-parent favouring
his/her own child.
- Rivalry between natural and step-children.
- Divided loyalties.
- Visits to the other parent/new partner. The child may be
unsettled before or after the visit, particularly if each
parent has a very different approach to caring/discipline,
or if there is jealousy or ill-feeling between the natural
parents.
- The arrival of a new baby.

It is important that you do not show any favouritism, even
though you will probably have more loyalty to the children you
look after the most. Try to be impartial and consistent in all the
decisions you have to make.

Be prepared to listen to the children's problems and be
supportive and understanding; allow them time and space for
this — since you are not part of the family you are in a good
position to listen.

VISITING: The child may require some help and understanding
if he is going to visit his other parent, both before and after the

visit. Ask your employers how they handle the situation and what they would like you to do and say. Do not forget that the children left behind may also need help in understanding what is happening.

VISITS BY STEPCHILDREN: As the children's nanny you will play an important role, if the stepchildren are coming to stay. Before they arrive you can help prepare your charges by talking to them and answering their questions. The stepchildren may feel and be greeted by a mixture of excitement, love, jealousy and resentment.

You may find it harder to have authority over the children you do not look after all the time. You may feel that you do not have them long enough to form a good working relationship, or to establish a routine — so you will have to start again each time they visit, rather as if you were starting a new job.

See also: Divorce, Extra Children, Older Children, Questions

Christine Atkinson, *Step-Parenting* (Thorsons).
Includes case histories, outlines problems, and offers solutions.

Stephen Collins, *Step-Parents* (Condor).
Helps with understanding the adults and children in this situation with legal and practical advice.

Annalena McAfee and Anthony Browne, *The Visitors Who Came to Stay* (Hamish Hamilton).
For four- to eight-year-olds. The father's girlfriend and son arrive.

Angela Grunsell, *Stepfamilies* (Franklin Watts).
Suitable for children aged six plus. Helps to explain and answer questions.

The National Stepfamily Association,
162 Tenison Road,
Cambridge
Tel: 0223 460 312 (Office)
      0223 460 313 (Counselling)

Stepfamily
76 Willesden Lane,
London NW6 7TA
Tel: 071 372 0844 (Office)
      071 372 0846
Their aim is to provide practical support and advice to
stepfamilies.

Tax and National Insurance

One of the worst aspects of employing a nanny is dealing with her tax and National Insurance contributions; unless you are a qualified accountant or have a perverse love of form filling, you will not look forward to the task. However you are required by law to pay tax and National Insurance contributions if your nanny earns more than the lower earnings limits for tax and National Insurance contributions. These change yearly – your tax / DSS office can tell you what they are.

If you do not operate this scheme your nanny may lose her entitlement to sick pay, unemployment and maternity benefit and ultimately her state pension. It is important therefore that it is done properly. You will pay her tax and both employers' and employees' National Insurance contributions. These payments are paid on her gross salary, leaving her the net salary which you will have discussed and agreed at the interview.

Before your nanny starts work for you, contact the tax office which deals with your area; nannies are employed under the simplified domestic PAYE scheme which is slightly easier to operate than a normal PAYE scheme, in theory anyway. Your tax office will send you:

- P30BC(Z) (Book of Payslips).
- P12 (Simplified Deduction card).
- P16 (Instructions telling you how to use it and simplified tax tables).
- CF391 (Non Contracted-Out National Insurance contributions, with the current tax year's contributions and weekly tables).

– NP15 (Employer's Guide to National Insurance contributions, available at your local DSS office if the tax office does not have it).

You will also get the tax district number, a Q reference, an accounts office reference and your nanny's tax code, all of which you will need when filling in the deductions card and pay slips.

If your nanny has a P45 from her previous job you should ignore it and send it to the tax office; under the Simplified Domestic Scheme used for employing nannies, a P45 is not necessary.

Each quarter you fill in the Simplified Deductions card with her net wage, which is her gross wage less tax and National Insurance contributions. It is usual to give your nanny a monthly pay slip with her wages, with details of her earnings and deductions, and best to fill in the Simplified Deductions card each month rather than wait for the quarter. If you are baffled by the documentation go and see your local tax officer and ask him to explain what you have to do to operate the Simplified Deductions scheme, particularly filling in the card.

At the end of each financial year you will fill in a P37 and return it to the tax office; you will be sent a new card and tax code for your nanny for the forthcoming year. You should also give your nanny a P60 which is a record of wages and deductions for the year.

When she leaves, send the tax office her Simplified Deductions card.

SELF-EMPLOYED NANNIES: Before employing a nanny on a self-employed basis you should check with the tax office that this is in order; if you leave her to pay her own tax and she fails to do so you will be responsible for her unpaid tax bill. The Inland Revenue does not usually allow self-employed status for nannies.

EMPLOYING NANNIES THROUGH COMPANIES: Some employers employ their nanny through their companies as secretaries; this reduces the amount of tax they pay on their profits.

However, if their company has more than five employees, the employees are entitled to maternity benefits and redundancy payments where relevant; and should they drive a company car this will be subject to tax. Both nanny and employer should be aware of these points.

 You may be fortunate enough to work for an employer who is happy to declare your full wages and pay your income tax and National Insurance contributions accordingly. However it is common practice for your employer to declare only part of your income to the Inland Revenue – this saves her money on your tax bill and she may therefore be able to offer you a slightly higher wage. If this is discovered both you and your employer could be prosecuted for the unpaid tax.

You should also be aware that if your employer declares less than the Lower Earnings Limit (the minimum wage you can earn before paying tax and National Insurance contributions), you may not qualify for full state benefits when you need them (pension, maternity, unemployment and sick pay).

It is your responsibility to make sure that your tax and insurance contributions are being paid. Unfortunately, some nannies discover too late that they have worked for an employer who has not paid their tax and National Insurance contributions. If you suspect that this might be happening to you, you can ring your tax office to confirm that your tax and National Insurance contributions are being paid. Your employer is obliged by law to pay your tax and NI contributions and should issue you with a monthly or weekly payslip with a record of your gross and net salary.

See also: Costs/Expenses, Interviews, Wages

Mary Beard, *Good Working Mothers' Guide* (Duckworths).
Includes a chapter on the formalities of employment.

DSS Social Security Advice Line for Employers
Freephone: 0800 393 539
Gives advice on all DSS matters.

Telephone

This subject is hardly ever discussed at the interview but it is probably one of the main reasons for employer / nanny friction. You are probably not aware of the size of the telephone bill you are contributing to and, unless your employer tells you, you may well not realise how important this is to her.

It is a rare nanny who does not use her employer's telephone to talk to her friends. However, remember that there will be a bill to be paid and you will be there when it arrives; your employer may well be unhappy if it is enormous.

You will also give a bad impression if you block the line when she is working from home or if she tries to call you from work and you are engaged every time — her trust in you will be undermined.

With each telephone call you make, ask yourself:

- Are the children safe and happy?
- Is the call absolutely necessary?
- Will you see the person during that day?
- Does the person telephone you? Will he or she ring you later anyway?
- Is it the cheapest time to ring?
- How much is it costing?

I was once offered £10 if the phone bill came in under £100. I got the money and my employer saved hers.

→ Quick Tip: Understand how the answerphone works and use it − put it on when you go out, and pass on your employer's messages.

 The telephone bill comes at the top of the list of employers' complaints about nannies. Few nannies think about the fact that you are paying for their calls and a large telephone bill may well make you angry and dismayed, particularly if you are careful with the bills.

- Decide what sort of an increase you are prepared to cope with. It is better to *expect* your phone bill to be larger than it was before you employed a nanny; apart from calls in connection with her job (which will include calls to and from other nannies making arrangements), allow her a reasonable amount of leeway with her own calls, particularly if she is a live-in nanny.
- When she first comes, and you are showing her the ropes, discuss the telephone, answerphone and message procedures and give her guidelines regarding her own calls. You could ask her to phone at cheap time where possible and to keep her calls short.
- When the bill is exorbitant, whilst you may hesitate to

make a fuss, if it is important to you, tell her and remind her pleasantly what you expect. If you do not speak up, she will have no way of knowing that you are not happy and will assume that all is well.

See also: Communication, Costs

Peak Rate:	Mon—Fri 9 am—1 pm
Standard Rate:	Mon—Fri 8 am—9 am and 1 pm—6 pm.
Cheap Rate:	Mon—Fri 6 pm—8 am and all weekend.
International:	See the telephone book or British Telecom leaflet, 'Your Guide to Telephone Charges'; or dial 100 and ask for 'Freefone B.T.I.'

Television

Television is an essential interview topic; your nanny's attitude to television, children's programmes, and her perception of what is and is not suitable for your age child will give you an idea how she may use it. Whatever your feelings about your children's use of television, you will need to make these clear at the interview and be happy that your nanny will respect them.

Attitudes vary enormously; some mums feel television is a negative influence, that their children are better off creating their own activities, that they may see something on TV that they are unable to cope with emotionally or intellectually, or that their behaviour will reflect what they watch. Others feel that, used with care, and as one of a number of other activities, TV is a magical, educational, exciting and informative medium which contributes to children's experiences of life in a positive way.

In between are the majority of mothers who regard television as part of life and do not have any strong feelings about it in relation to their children either way.

Whatever your view, you will need to be sure that your nanny will be prepared to do as you ask and respect your wishes. Avoid double standards – do not allow your children to watch more than you allow your nanny to allow your children to watch. If you do your nanny will not take your feelings seriously and she will be greeted with cries of 'Mummy lets me' when she tries to carry out your wishes.

VIDEOS: Be wary of your children seeing unsuitable videos in other people's houses when you are not in control; you may need to ask your nanny to keep an eye on what your children do at other people's houses.

You will be told at the interview what the parents like the children to watch and should be ready for them to ask you your views too. You may find that their attitude is different to yours – be prepared to carry out their wishes. The most usual situation is to have a limited time for children to watch television. You may be asked to watch with them.

Restricting the children's viewing can be an uphill struggle – and you may feel that your employer does not fully appreciate it, since she does not have to handle the situation on a daily basis in school time. It will help if you establish the rules early on in your job, allow time for the television in your routine, and find workable strategies for turning it off which are appropriate to the child and the family.

> *Helen was having serious behavioural problems with her two charges and could not work out why; she finally discovered that the whole of playtime at school revolved around* Neighbours, *which their mother had forbidden them to watch. They were therefore being left out of all the playgroup games. Helen discussed the problem with her employer who relented, on the understanding that she watched it with the children. Helen is now hooked too.*

Your employer may be prepared to be more flexible about the use of television with the children if she sees that you have a responsible attitude to it and that you do a variety of other activities with the children as well.

 Quick Tip: Make sure they are watching what you think they are watching!

Many nannies have a television in their room, sometimes provided by the employers. If you do not have one, (and like to watch programmes) it is a good investment to purchase one for yourself, as sharing the family's TV is not easy and you will find you cannot relax properly and do not get a break from the family, nor they you. When babysitting, looking after a baby or if the children are out, you may like to have the television on for company. Therefore if the family does not have a TV, be sure you can survive without one.

See also: Activities, Interviews, Questions

 Maire Messenger Davies, *Television Is Good For Your Kids* (Hilary Shipman)

Betsy Byars, *The TV Kid* (Bodley Head).
Lennie is unable to move his eyes from the TV set.

British Action for Children's Television,
21 Stephen Street,
London W1P 1PL
Tel: 071 255 1444
A group of concerned parents, broadcasters and
teachers who are campaigning for 'quality and
diversity' in children's television.

Toys

 A nanny's duties will include the care and repair of the
children's toys and books, and keeping the area they are
stored in tidy and organised.

- Encourage the children to help you do this; turning the
  task into a game or activity will help.
- Teach them the value of respecting their things from an
  early age.
- Teach the children to take care with other children's toys
  when you are out.
- Make sure your friends' charges are not guilty of abusing
  your charges' toys when they come to play.
- Maintain their interest in their toys by constantly changing what is available to them.
- Make sure the toys and books are appropriate to their age
  and ability.
- Provide various types of toys including craft toys, outside
  toys, and toys you can make or improvise from household
  objects.
- Tidy the toys / playroom regularly, either daily or once a
  week. You will have to do this, even if your employer
  does not when you are not there, however soul-destroying
  this may be.

– Sort the toys out every now and again but, because children are sensitive about their possessions and where they are kept, be tactful about what they see you doing.
– Put the batteries back in the laser gun and musical train at least once a month!

Quick Tip: Do not be tempted to move too much around in one go or too soon after starting a job.

Keeping the toys clean, tidy and usable is repetitive and thankless; however, since incomplete and broken toys are rarely enjoyed or used, this is an important part of your nanny's routine. Make it clear to her at the beginning what you expect; she will set her standards by whether or not she thinks you have noticed and it will be much harder to ask her to change once a pattern has been established. It is a good idea to show her you have noticed the effort she makes and thank her when appropriate.

Quick Tip: Leave the playroom or toy cupboard as you would hope to find it.

See also: Activities, Duties

The National Toy Libraries Association,
68 Church Way,
London NW1 1LT
Tel: 071 387 9592
Can supply you with details of your local toy library.

Training

'My training gave me confidence, experience and knowledge, which I would not have had without it.'

'I've been nannying for four years and know as much if not more than any trained nanny.'

'I feel more confident with a trained nanny — and feel that you get what you pay for.'

'I employ the person not the qualifications.'

Whatever your feelings about training, qualifications can only improve your status when you are going for interviews and will also ensure that you have the basic skills for the job. There are many courses available to anyone wishing to train to become a nanny which vary in content, length, entry requirements, and the qualification gained. Although most are for the training of nursery nurses in the public sector, they do cover most of what you need to know to be a nanny. Before deciding on a course you need to be aware of what each one offers.

Courses vary from county to county and change constantly; you can get information on courses from your local colleges, job centres, libraries or from your school.

TRAINING OPTIONS

Local Authority Colleges:
National Nursery Examination Board. Diploma in Nursery Nursing (NNEB). This is a two-year course for students aged sixteen years and over. There are no specific entry requirements and colleges vary; some require two or three good GCSE passes including English, others have their own entrance exam, and all will take account of a student's personality, experience, ability and commitment to child care. The course is a combination of theory and practical work in caring for children from birth up to seven years old. The theory includes child care, child development, health, first aid, nutrition, social studies, music, art, craft and drama, man and his environment. The practical placements include: families, hospitals, (maternity or special care baby units), nursery schools, infant schools and at special needs schools / centres.

SCOTVEC National Certificate in Nursing (SNNEB). The Scottish equivalent to the NNEB.

National Association of Maternal and Child Welfare (NAMCW), Nursery Nurses Diploma. This course is for students aged sixteen plus and is a two-year full-time course. Entry requirements vary according to the college, but GCSE level Maths and English are often looked for. It may be studied at colleges including sixth form and through employment training schemes. The syllabus includes a study of child care, health, illness and disease, and emotional, physical, social and intellectual development. Play activities, special needs and sociology of the family, up to and including adolescence, are also studied. The students also gain practical experience with work-place assessments.

BTEC National Certificate or Diploma in Caring (Nursery Nursing). Minimum age for this course is sixteen and entry requirements are four GCSEs (grades A−C), or a good standard in CPVE (Certificate of Pre-Vocational Education), or a BTEC first award in a relevant subject. Personality and interest in child care are also taken into account. The course is full-time and for two years, with college-based study and practical work experience in establishments including hospitals, schools, nurseries and voluntary organisations. Students cover a wide range of subjects including child care, child development, community health, creative studies, special needs, safety and first aid and data investigation.

City and Guilds Scheme No 331−1, Family and Community Care Course. Entry requirements are minimum age of sixteen years with some GCSE passes and a genuine interest in people. The course is full-time for two years and includes first aid, caring skills, cooking and nutrition, human growth and development, social studies and art and craft. Practical placement experience is with families and in the community.

There are several other courses that include caring skills but the above is the most appropriate to working as a nanny.

<u>The Isle College, Wisbech; Nannies.</u> This is a one-year course specifically for training nannies. Entry requirements are at least three GCSE passes of grade E or above. Personal qualities are also taken into account. The course involves theory of child development, play, first aid, care of the sick, social studies, biology and communication. The practical placements are one day a week at private homes, sometimes for longer if the placement is to be residential.

Private Colleges:

<u>Norland Nursery Training College.</u> The NNEB, the RSH (Royal Society of Health) Diploma of Nursery Nursing and the Norland Diploma are awarded to students upon passing the course. This residential college takes students aged eighteen years and over who have at least three GCSE (or equivalent) passes at grade C or above; one must be in English Language. The course includes NNEB studies and lasts two years, with an additional nine months' probationary period in a residential family post.

<u>The Princess Christian College.</u> The NNEB, RSH and the Princess Christian Certificate are awarded here. To attend you have to be aged seventeen and a half or over, with three GCSE (or equivalent) passes grade C or above, (one must be in English). The course includes NNEB studies, lasts for two years, and is residential.

<u>The Chiltern Nursery Training College.</u> (NNEB and the RSH.) Entry requirements are GCSE (or equivalent) passes in at least three subjects including English Language. You also have to be aged eighteen years or over. This residential course is for two years and includes NNEB coursework. There is also a one-year course in practical child care, which is less academic.

<u>The London Montessori Centre.</u> (NNEB and The Montessori Nursery (foundation) Teaching Diploma. NFTD.) Entry requirements are at least three GCSEs including English, and you need to be aged seventeen years or over. This course is

non-residential and is for two years. It covers the NNEB syllabus and the NFTD, which is similar but includes the Montessori method of education.

<u>Certificate in Nannying</u>. This is an alternative one-year course. The students earn while they study by working for a family for a small amount per week, and have time off to study at the centre.

Some private colleges also act as agencies for their qualified students and place them before they have finished their training.

BEFORE TRAINING: Once you have been accepted on to a course, you can help yourself by:

- Going to college open days, where you may be able to talk to past students and look at their work.
- Getting experience in looking after children, perhaps by babysitting or weekend childminding.
- Looking at some child care books and magazines, and familiarising yourself with the current topics.

DURING TRAINING: You will be acquiring many skills that can be used and adapted to working as a nanny. It is a good idea to talk to other nannies and where possible employers of nannies, to help you decide if nannying is for you. Once you are sure, you can then start to decide on the type of job you think you might like when you leave college. Have a look at job advertisements to see the kind of jobs on offer.

There are good untrained nannies and bad trained ones; there are employers who swear by trained nannies and will not employ anyone else and there are those who do not rate the training courses on offer. There is always fierce debate on the merits of training amongst nannies, who defend their qualifications or experience.

Some courses are more appropriate to being a nanny than others; if you are concerned to employ a nanny with relevant training, it is worth researching exactly what she has studied on her training course and not just ask her for the name of the course.

A 'good nanny' is a combination of knowledge, experience, attitude, personality, commitment, and whether or not she suits your particular needs, children and family. Training may provide some or all of these qualifications.

See also: Interviews, First Job / First Nanny, Type of Job

 B/TEC The Business and Technical Education
Council
Central House,
Upper Woburn Place,
London WC1H OHH
Tel: 071 387 4141

Chiltern Nursery Training College
16 Peppard Road,
Caversham,
Reading,
Berkshire RG4 8JZ
Tel: 0734 471847 / 471131

City and Guilds of London Institute
76 Portland Place,
London W1N 4AA
Tel: 071 580 3050 (Headquarters)
     071 278 2468 (Department Offices)

Isle College
Ramnoth Road,
Wisbech,
Cambridgeshire PE13 2JE
Tel: 0945 582561

London Montessori Centre
18 Balderton Street,
London W1Y 1TG
Tel: 071 493 0165
One of the larger training centres.

National Association for Maternal and Child Welfare
1 South Audley Street,
London W1Y 6JS
Tel: 071 491 2772

National Nursery Examination Board (NNEB)
8 Chequer Street,
St Albans,
Hertfordshire AL1 3XZ
Tel: 0727 867333

Norland Nursery Training College
Denford Park,
Hungerford,
Berkshire RG17 OPQ
Tel: 0488 82252

Princess Christian College,
26 Wilbraham Road,
Fallowfield,
Manchester M14 6JX
Tel: 061 224 4560

Scottish Nursery Nurses Examination Board
6 Kilnford Crescent,
Dundonald,
Kilmarnock,
Ayrshire KA2 9DW

Twins or More

 You will need a competent, confident and calm nanny to cope with twins well, especially if they are very young and particularly if she is to be in sole charge; you will also need to pay her more than if she only had one child to look after. At the interview, find out if she is completely aware of what looking after your twins actually means; a few questions about routine, feeding and getting around will give you an idea. Since you may have to share more of the care than usual with your nanny, particularly at night, it is important that you get on well with her.

Looking after twins is challenging, rewarding and hard work! At the interview you will need to find out the parents' approach to caring for their children and satisfy yourself that you will be able to work with them happily. The job will vary according to the age of the children — make sure you fully understand what you are being asked to do.

In families that consist of a lot of children, particularly of the same age, you may find you have to share the job with one of the parents or perhaps another nanny. If this is so, make sure that you meet them first and are happy to work with them.

Before taking a job with twins or more you should consider:

- You will need to be very organised and have a good routine, particularly when they are babies. For example you will need to establish the same sleep / wake / feed patterns in order to give yourself enough time to cope.
- You will have to meet the individual needs of each child: twins often get treated as if they are the same, or they get treated as a pair, when they are usually very different and need to be treated as such.
- You will have to make sure you cater for the needs of other children in the family — twins tend to dominate and problems arise if the other children feel left out.
- Twins attract a lot of attention from outsiders. Both they and other siblings may need help coping with it.
- You will not be able to get out and about so easily. Taking a lot of children shopping, or on buses and trains, is not always easy.
- You will need to be able to drive.
- You will need to find and maintain two or more sets of friends. People's attitudes vary; two or more children are not always as welcome as one since they are harder to accommodate. If this is so you will need to make an extra effort to build up a social life for the children and yourself during the day. The family's health visitor may know of other nannies in similar circumstances who may be able to give you some helpful hints.

For help and advice on how to cope with twins and more, and on how to find others in the same situation, the books and organisations listed below may help:

Elizabeth Friedrich and Cherry Rowland, *The Twins Handbook* (Robson).
Guide for parents, covering the first five years.

Jan Needle *Springy and Sam*, *Mad Scramble*, *As Seen on TV*. (Heinemann).
Three books on the adventures of twins.

Averil Clegg and Anne Woollett, *Twins* (Young Library).
Everything about being and looking after twins.

Twins and Multiple Births Association (Tamba)
Sheila Payne (Secretary)
59 Sunnyside, Worksop,
Nottinghamshire S81 7LN
Contact for family-to-family support and to find your local branch.

The Multiple Births Foundation
Institute of Obstetrics and Gynaecology,
Queen Charlotte's & Chelsea Hospital,
Goldhawk Road, London W6 OXG
Tel: 081 748 4666 Ext 5201
Contact for family to professional help. Advice given on medical subjects.

Type of Job

We have looked at the main terms and conditions that affect a job elsewhere, for example, duties, accommodation, wages, hours and holidays. This section looks at how a job changes according to the jobs of the parents and the number, sex and ages of the children.

Types of Nanny

Nanny	Mother's Help
Live in or out. Trained or untrained but experienced, nursery duties only, earns more than other kinds of carer and often has sole charge.	Live in or out. Usually works with mother, and is untrained; duties include housework or any other task which mother needs help with; earns less than a nanny.

Au Pair	Maternity Nurse
Live in. Foreign. In the country to learn the language. Only works five hours a day; often attends college part time. Earns very little but all is provided.	Live in. Highly paid. Specialises in the care of mother and baby in the first few weeks. They are very often mature and experienced.

Type of Job

MOTHER AND FATHER AT WORK (SOLE CHARGE)
Both parents at work full time or away for regular periods; most nannies prefer this, particularly if they are experienced.

MOTHER OR FATHER AT HOME

Not Working

You may feel constantly watched and under pressure to perform your duties well all the time.

It can be difficult to delegate completely; no nanny ever does things exactly as you would and if you are there to see this it can be difficult

Mother can intervene and undermine your authority.

Children can be difficult because they can play you off against their mother.

It may be difficult to relax or feel that you can go out; friends feel uncomfortable visiting when your employer is at home which can contribute to loneliness.

to sit back and let her do the job, particularly if you are unable to get away from her and the children in the house.

It is important to back each other up particularly with discipline.

Clear lines of delegation are important if this situation is to work satisfactorily.

You have more control over what your nanny is doing and can actually see what the children are doing or eating.

Have you got a JUMBOSIZE stair gate? It's not to keep him in... it's to keep his Mother OUT

Babycare

Try and discuss your plans for the week with your employer — you may be able to work round each other.

You have more time to discuss things with your employer.

Give your nanny an opportunity to have visitors when you are not at home and tell her when you want to be on your own in the house.

Working

As well as the above points, you will also need to consider the following:

You spend a lot of time stopping the children interrupting the mother.

You can usually leave on time.

It can be hard to concentrate if you can hear the children crying, fighting or laughing in a nearby room. It is important to develop the ability to ignore the domestic situation.

Have set times of the day when you join the family then everyone knows where they stand and your nanny does not feel that her every move is being monitored. You will also feel less left out. You do not waste time and energy travelling.

SHARE A NANNY

One nanny or mother's help works for two employers or more and looks after all the children; houses, facilities, car and costs are all shared and the employers decide on the financial arrangements between them, including who pays the tax and National Insurance contributions.

CHILDREN

The number, age and sex of the children will affect your choice of job and your choice of nanny.

Two children:

- The most usual situation, and even if the age gap is large, it is usually possible to accommodate both children's needs without too much difficulty.
- Depending on their ages they will be able to keep each other company.
- You may have to cope with rivalry, jealousy and fighting.
- The older one is often able to help with the younger one.

More than two children:

When considering a job with two or more children you will need to be aware of the above points and also:

- The more children there are the more interesting and stimulating the job. However, it may be more difficult to do activities with all the children together because of their individual needs and stages of development.
- It is physically more difficult, particularly when the children are young, for example, there is more washing and ironing, and more equipment and clothes to organise.
- You may need a computer to organise their activities and social life!

Whilst most nannies prefer to look after two children, it can be more difficult to find a nanny for more than two, and will probably mean paying more. You will be more stretched for time the more children there are, and will therefore probably rely more heavily on your nanny to keep things running smoothly. You will need a strong, competent and unruffled nanny who is happy to cope with the workload of several children.

AGE GAP

Depending on the age and sex of the children, the age gap can make a great deal of difference to the job; you will need to consider the individual needs of the children and the implications of their difference in age; for example, if you have a seven- and five-year-old you may have to cope with their fighting, but you will be able to read them the same stories, feed them the same food, and their daily routine will be very similar. If, for example, you have a one-year-old and a five-year-old you will have time for each of them on their own but you will have to fit the older child's activities round the younger one's routine, take the younger one with you when you go out with the older one, and so on (a nightmare for swimming lessons!)

A good, motivated nanny who genuinely enjoys children will have no difficulty taking on different ages and age gaps. However, if you are in any doubt it may help to employ a nanny who has experience of the particular age and age gap of your children — if she has, she will have first-hand knowledge of the problems relevant to that age and will therefore deal with them better.

See also: Babies, Duties, Extra Children, First Job, New Job / New Nanny, Only Child, Older Children, One-Parent Families, Special Needs, Stepchildren, Training, Twins, Wages

---

Judith Humphries and Julia Allen, *Working with Children and Young People* (Kogan Page).
A career book explaining the types of job in this field and the qualifications required.

Working Mothers Association,
77 Holloway Road,
London N7
Tel: 071 700 5771
A self-help organisation providing support, advice and information to its members.

Unions

The Professional Association of Nursery Nurses (PANN) helps qualified nursery nurses working as nannies in the private sector and handles cases on their behalf; members are covered by their insurance scheme.

Trained nursery nurses and nannies can also join the National Association of Government Officers (NALGO) or the National Union of Public Employees (NUPE).

See also: Insurance, Leaving

 Professional Association of Nursery Nurses (PANN),
St James Court,
77 Friar Gate,
Derby DE1 1EZ
Tel: 0332 43029

National Association of Local Government Officers (NALGO),
1 Mabledon Place,
London WC1
Tel: 071 388 2366

National Union of Public Employees (NUPE),
Civic House,
20 Grand Depot Road,
London SE18 6SF
Tel: 081 854 2244

Wages

RATES

Wages vary enormously and depend on:

- The type of job, e.g. number of children, duties, hours, live in / out.
- The type of employer.
- The part of the country.
- Any other perks, e.g. car, holidays, accommodation.
- The qualifications / experience of the nanny.

GUIDE TO WAGES

	Net Weekly Pay	
	Live In £	Live Out £
Experienced mature NNEB / Norlander:	100 – 125+	125 – 150+
NNEB 1st job:	80 – 100	120 – 125
Mother's Help (unqualified)	50 – 80	80 – 100

Net is after deductions of income tax and National Insurance contributions. When discussing wages, it is usual to deal in the net rather than the gross figure.

Since there is no fixed pay scale, you must be realistic about what you can earn; if you are eighteen, untrained, with only one previous job, don't expect to earn what a twenty-eight-year-old, very experienced NNEB will earn. As with all jobs, you earn more as you gain experience and — although not always — according to your qualifications.

Agencies will tell you what you might expect to earn in your area but remember that they may not necessarily find you a job which pays the figure that they have quoted you. Talk to other nannies if you can, look in newspapers and magazines and ask your college tutors for advice.

It is important to clarify your wages before you accept the job since it will be more difficult to bring it up once you have started work and got to know the family. Ask about your wages at the interview after you have found out about the other details of the job. It does not give a good impression to make it your first question, since your priorities should be with the children. Do not be afraid to ask for what you feel you are worth; a job rarely works out well if you are unhappy with your wages. However, you will need to take into account the family, the perks, the hours and the conditions as well as the money when choosing a job, since these are often as important as the amount you earn.

'Right. You'll be paid in postage stamps with all the tap water you can drink thrown in. Does that sound fair?'

METHOD OF PAYMENT: It is important to clarify frequency and method of payment; monthly in arrears is normal and probably fits in with your employer's work situation. It is amazing how many employers 'forget' to pay you on time. Try and have an arrangement which prevents this:

- Standing Order: Your employer makes an arrangement with her bank to regularly pay you a set amount each month on a certain day, generally the day after she gets paid herself. You may like to arrange to have the bank send you a regular statement if you are paid this way so that you can check how much is going into your account.
- Cheque.
- Cash.
- Combination of cheque and cash.

You will need to agree on a day or date each month for payment. If your employer persistently forgets or is late paying you, try one of the following:

- Make a note on the family calendar.
- Remind your employer at the beginning of the week you are due to be paid.

Your employer is responsible for payment of tax and National Insurance contributions on your behalf. Employers do not get any relief on payment of your tax and consequently many of them prefer to declare some of your salary for tax and pay the rest as expenses. This reduces the amount of tax both you and your employer are liable for, and gives you more money in your hand and your employer less of a tax bill. For example, on £100 per week gross you / your employer may pay tax on £65 and have £35 cash in hand.

PAYSLIPS: Your employer should give you payslips with each wage packet which have an accurate record of your earnings and deductions. At the end of each financial year you should be given a P60 which is a record of your earnings for that year.

Do not forget to pay your nanny regularly and correctly; not being paid on time or the right amount is one of the 'little' things which can grow into a big issue for a nanny since it says to her that you do not value or respect her.

If you are unsure how much you should pay your nanny you can ask other employers in your area, but make sure you are comparing like with like. You will want to take into account the age and experience of the nanny, how badly you want her, and what else you can offer her – car, time off, perks, holidays, accommodation, and of course how much you can afford, before deciding on her wage.

You may feel that it is worth the expense of an accountant to deal with the administration of your nanny's wages, tax and National Insurance contributions. Fees vary for this service, largely according to the size of your accountant's firm and therefore his overheads.

RISES

Most jobs have a pay review structure, and, depending on the economic climate, this is usually yearly. It also relates to performance.

Discussing money is one of the most difficult things to do but if you feel that you deserve a rise, do not be afraid to ask for one. You may find you are working for an employer who never offers a rise and hopes that you will not ask. If this is the case, choose a good moment (perhaps when you are sorting out other daily expenses), take a deep breath and do not stop! You might say something like 'While we're on the subject of money, could we discuss my wages?' You may well be asked to say how much you want – think this out beforehand; your employer may offer you an extra perk instead of (or as well as) a rise.

When your nanny asks for a rise you may feel embarrassment at not even having thought of it; despair that you will have to find yet more money; or indignant that she has dared to ask.

You may work for a company which offers an annual pay review as a matter of course; nannies are at the mercy of the good will of their employers. The temptation is to prioritise everything but the nanny but if you value your nanny, you can only improve your relationship with her by offering a rise before she asks you for one.

See also: Banks / Building Societies, Communication, Illness, Interview, Pregnancy, Tax and National Insurance, Type of Job

---

Weekends

Few nannies want to work every weekend and most will try to find jobs without weekend work. Therefore, if you want a choice of nanny, you are better off not asking her to work weekends, or asking her to work a limited number each year, and trying to compensate for them in some other way.

Some nannies are happy to work at weekends if they are given the choice not to — you could make weekends a separate issue entirely with separate terms and conditions, or give your nanny first option but have alternative arrangements as a back-up if at all possible.

If you do employ a nanny who works at the weekend you will:

- Have a babysitter at the point of the week where you probably need one most.
- Be free to pursue your own activities and go away when you want to.
- Have an extra pair of hands if the size of your household is large enough to need it.

On the other hand you will:

- Have little privacy.

- Possibly find it hard with regard to discipline of the children since they will have both carers around at the same time.
- Not have much time to get to know your children on your own.

At the interview be sure to be clear about what you expect your nanny to do at weekends and how she is expected to fit in, whether she is working or simply staying in the house. Each week, if possible, tell her your plans for the weekend so that she can work round you with her social life. This will make both parties feel more comfortable.

Before you go for a job interview decide on how you feel about working weekends. If you are happy with the other conditions of the job you may choose to be flexible over weekend work. However, make sure you have thought this through thoroughly. If you are the kind of person who likes to go out, go away or is used to having the weekends free, do not assume that you will get used to working at the weekends — you probably won't, and will eventually resent it. If you are offered two weekdays off instead you need to think carefully — you will be off but your friends and family may well be working or busy and unable to spend time or go out with you.

Before taking a job that involves weekends you need to clarify the following points:

- How often will you be required to work?
- Is it part of the job or will you be paid extra?
- Will you get days off in lieu, and if so, when?
- What duties will you have? Will you be babysitting or on duty all day?

These points should be included in your contract or side letter. It may also be useful to ask:

- What your routine will be.

– What the children do.
– Whether the parents will be present too.

Working at the weekends will be very different to working during the week; the parents and children are not in a work routine and the rules will undoubtedly change from those you apply during the week. You will have to be flexible and work out what the 'weekend' standards are; it may be difficult to see the children behaving very differently at the weekends and not be able to do as you would do during the week since you are no longer in sole charge.

A live-in nanny not working at the weekend may find the situation quite difficult. To help avoid the feeling of awkwardness and embarrassment it is a good idea to find out what is expected of you. You may be able to find out from the previous nanny. If not, ask your employer if there are any particular dos and don'ts they would like you to observe, what areas of the house you can use and if friends can visit. Once you have experienced a few weekends you will learn the best times to keep, the best actions to take and will hopefully get into a routine you feel comfortable with. You will need to try and keep out of the way as much as you can and not get involved in the family's time together unless invited.

Make sure that you do not undermine your employers' authority at the weekends since the children will probably still come to you if you are in the house. Refer them back to their parents and explain that you are not looking after them that day.

Most nannies, if they are able to, choose to go away at weekends, to avoid the above problems and to get a break from the family and house. Be sure to tell your employers exactly when you are coming back after a weekend away and let them know if this changes for any reason. It is important that you do get back on time and are fit and able to do your job. It is sensible to tell your employers where you are going and perhaps who with, although you are not obliged to do so.

See also: Interviews, Privacy, Social Life

Working Abroad

If you are going to work and reside abroad with your family for long periods you will need a confident, cheerful person who can cope with living in a foreign environment, using a foreign language, and dealing with the problems of looking after children in an unfamiliar place. You may decide to take your existing nanny with you, provided you think that she would cope, is happy to come and does not have ties at home which would make her miserable if she did so.

If, however, you decide to advertise for a new nanny, you will receive a lot of interest for the job and will need to vet the applicants very carefully, checking their motives for wanting the job and commitment to it. Be sure that the applicant does not just want free passage to sunny climes! A lot of girls become nannies simply to enable them to travel. It will be important to keep your nanny for the period you are abroad since replacing her long distance, even with the help of agencies, will not be easy or cheap.

At the interview it will be helpful to find out:

- Whether she enjoys travel, has any knowledge of the place you are going to, would be prepared to get to know the country and its customs, if relevant, could cope with any homesickness or loneliness, and enjoys good health.
- How long she intends staying with you. You might ask for a commitment in writing.
- What experience she has of foreign travel.

Try to give your nanny a realistic picture of what she might expect from the country and your immediate circumstances; give her as much information as possible so that she knows what she is letting herself in for in taking the job.

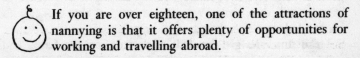

If you are over eighteen, one of the attractions of nannying is that it offers plenty of opportunities for working and travelling abroad.

Should the family you are working for ask you to go abroad with them make sure that you are happy in that job — a change of country will not change your feelings if you are not. You may be looking for a job abroad on your own account; if so, there are many agencies who place nannies abroad and many advertisements appear in newspapers and magazines, so you will have a lot of possibilities.

Using an agency that specialises in placing nannies abroad can have advantages; they can offer you back-up should you need it in times of dispute, and many have other offers such as free insurance, tickets home and friendship circles abroad. The agency should check the family out for you and you should be happy that the information they give you on the family and the job is sufficient.

Whether you are going with your existing employer or with a new one, you will need to do some background research. Look in travel books and brochures, contact embassies, and if possible, talk to a nanny who has experience of working abroad. Before going any further ask yourself whether you think you can cope with the possible loneliness, different social customs, language, food, and so on.

You will also need to feel happy that you will be able to cope with the children: if they do not speak English, depending on their ages, you may have problems with communication and discipline. You will have to be prepared to learn the language quickly if you are to form a good relationship with them and have authority over them. You will also have to deal with any cultural differences, for example, food, routine, play, school and friends, and may face coping with servants who may resent you and whom the children love.

If you are going with your existing charges, depending on their ages you will be playing an important part in helping them adjust to their new lifestyle in a foreign country, whilst trying to adjust to it yourself! Expect them to feel insecure — help them to keep in touch with home whilst building a new circle of friends and activities. Preparing them for the move with books / videos before you go will help.

Make sure you get detailed information on the terms and

conditions being offered. As well as considering all the usual points for a nannying job you will need to have the following clarified and written into a contract:

WORK/RESIDENCE PERMITS/VISAS: You may require one or all of these; regulations vary according to the country and your length of stay. Find out early on what is needed and whether your employer will arrange it for you.

WAGES: What arrangements will there be for the payment of your wages? Will you be paid in the local currency or in English money?

TAX AND NATIONAL INSURANCE: How will they take care of your tax and National Insurance? It is particularly important that you clarify this. You can get advice from your local tax office regarding payment of income tax and contact the DSS Overseas Branch regarding your National Insurance contributions.

INSURANCE: Who will be responsible for your insurance? (Medical and Personal, Motor.)

DRIVING LICENCE: Will you be able to use your existing driving licence? If not, will your employer arrange whatever is necessary?

FARES: Who will be responsible for paying for your outward and return journey?

VISITS HOME: Will your employer pay for you to go home for a holiday, and how often?

LANGUAGE: Will your employer pay for you to learn the language?

Where appropriate it is also a good idea to ask to see photographs of the children, family, accommodation, house and area and if possible, a reference from a previous nanny.

If you are being interviewed in this country, either by agencies or by relatives, remember that these are not the people you will work for and your prospective employers may not be as good or bad.

Be prepared for an initial period of culture shock and homesickness as the situation you find yourself in may not be what you expected; allow yourself a settling-in period before making any major decisions.

Although working abroad sounds glamorous, and can be very successful, when a job goes wrong you are a long way from home with no one to help you; at worst, provided you have enough funds and your passport, you can simply come home. If you have a serious problem, contact your local British Embassy.

 Quick Tip: Lodge your passport and your return fare with the local British Embassy.

See also: Adverts, Agencies, Interviews, Leaving, Moving House

---

 Godfrey Golzen, *The Daily Telegraph Guide to Working Abroad* (Kogan Page).
A comprehensive guide which includes useful profiles of each country.

Roger Jones, *How to Get a Job Abroad* (How to Books Ltd).
Includes where to go and what to do before you go.

DSS Overseas Branch,
Newcastle Upon Tyne, NE98 1YX

British Council,
10 Spring Gardens,
London SW1A 2BN
Tel: 071 930 8466